Do You Love Me?

A Practical Guide to Catholic Prayer & Spirituality

by
Catholic Bishops' Conference of England & Wales

*All booklets are published thanks
to the generous support of the members
of the Catholic Truth Society*

CATHOLIC TRUTH SOCIETY
PUBLISHERS TO THE HOLY SEE

CTS Publications

CTS booklets explain the faith, teaching and life of the Catholic Church. They are based on Sacred Scripture, the Second Vatican Council documents, and the *Catechism of the Catholic Church*. Our booklets provide authentic Catholic teaching; they address issues of life and of truth which are relevant to all. They aim to inform and educate readers on the many issues that people have to deal with today.

In addition, CTS nurtures and supports the Christian life through its many spiritual, liturgical, educational and pastoral books. As Publisher to the Holy See, CTS publishes the official documents of the Catholic Church as they are issued.

website: www.CTSBooks.org

ISBN 978 1 78469 011 3

Contents

Jesus said to Simon Peter, *"Simon, son of John, do you love me more than these?"* Simon Peter answered him, *"Yes, Lord, you know that I love you."* Jesus said to him, *"Feed my lambs."* He then said to Simon Peter a second time, *"Simon, son of John, do you love me?"* Simon Peter answered him, *"Yes, Lord, you know that I love you."* Jesus said to him, *"Tend my sheep."* Jesus said to him the third time, *"Simon, son of John, do you love me?"* Peter was distressed that Jesus had said to him a third time, *"Do you love me?"* and he said to him, *"Lord, you know everything; you know that I love you"*. Jesus said to him, *"Feed my sheep"*. (*John* 21:1-19)

Foreword

I am very pleased to welcome this publication 'Do you love me'. I believe many will find in it great help in their life of prayer, in their lived relationship with our Blessed Lord. For this reason, it is a most important publication and I thank Bishop Brian Noble and all who worked with him in preparing and publishing this imaginative contribution to our lives.

Our relationship with Jesus, our life of prayer, is the back-bone of our life of faith. As his disciples each of us is called to know him better, to make more and more space for him in our hearts, to enter every day into intimate conversation with him. This interior life is a source of joy, of encouragement, of strength for each of us. In these pages we will find great help in deepening that life each day.

In our life of prayer, Our Blessed Lady, Mary the Mother of Jesus, plays a very special part. She is given to us as a precious guide in our journey to Jesus her Son. She is always wanting to bring us to him. She is always holding him out to us. I am pleased to seek her prayers and patronage for this publication.

Mary teaches us always to be attentive, to be listening for the whisper of God in our lives, for it was the Angel of the Lord who declared to Mary God's intention for her. She also teaches us not to be afraid to ask questions of God, "But how can this be?" Then she teaches us to be ready to follow. Her words should find an echo in our hearts each day: "Be it done to me according to your word". She is, indeed, the first and the best of all disciples.

Mary also teaches us to make our journey of faith and prayer within the context of the Church, in the company of our fellow disciples. We make this journey better together. So too this publication will yield its fruit more fully if it is used not only personally but also if the reading, reflections and prayer are shared. This can certainly be within a family or, of course, within a group of friends or groups of parishioners. I hope that many groups will find great encouragement here.

Mary also teaches us that all of this, every prayer that crosses our lips, comes as a gift of the Holy Spirit. It was the Holy Spirit who brought the Word of God into the flesh of Mary. So too in our lives. It is the Holy Spirit who not only confirms the goodness in our lives as a gift of God but also works to transform our lives, step by step, into a clearer witness to Christ and his Gospel.

The journey presented in this publication, then, always takes place, we pray, under the guidance, the gift, and the power of the Holy Spirit. May this publication help us all express more deeply and respond more fully to the powerful invitation "Do you love me?", Yes Lord, you know that I love you, help me to love you more and more.

✝ Cardinal Vincent Nichols,
President, Catholic Bishops' Conference of England & Wales

Introduction

The title of this book comes from the last chapter of the Gospel according to St John. It is the account of the conversation Jesus had with Peter after his resurrection. In that passage Jesus asks Peter the question *Do you love me?* It is a question which Christians down through the centuries have heard in their own hearts and it is addressed by the Lord to each one of us today. How do we grow a real and living relationship with him in the context of our world and our membership of the Church? What guidelines do we have to help us on this spiritual path and what resources are offered to us? *Do you love me?* is a different sort of publication to a normal book. Let us tell you what it is not! This is not a text book about spirituality. It is not a book about the Bible, although it is centred around the Gospel narrative which gives us the title. It is not a book which can be used only if you are a member of a parish group, although we've put some ideas in for that. It has a limited scope. It is not a summary of Christian doctrine or a book on the liturgy, though we see where that fits in to our spiritual path. So what is it?

So, *Do you love me?* is designed as a book for reflection. Catholic spirituality is something very active. It is something *we do*, not just something we read about. What we aim to do in this book is to offer you some guidelines, not only about what Catholic spirituality is, but also about how to develop your own relationship with God. It is this which lies at the heart of all living Catholic spirituality.

The place of the liturgy and sacramental life is clearly central for Catholics. The Mass is the "source and summit" of our life. In order to appreciate just how central it is this book focuses on the development of a personal relationship with Christ. It is our relationship with the living Lord which gives life to our celebration of the liturgy. Our part in the sacramental life of the Church will become ever richer and deeper as that relationship develops.

Catholic spirituality is too rich and deep to be encompassed in a single definition. It is so rich that it has not been possible to cover every single aspect of it in this publication. If something is not covered extensively in these pages it does *not* mean that it is unimportant. However, what is included takes us, we believe, to the heart of our spirituality and there are appropriate quotes from our rich tradition throughout the book to illustrate how our themes have been part of the Church's life for centuries.

How to use this book

As with all books, the temptation is to rush through it, reading quickly from one section to the next to see what each part contains. Resist the temptation! Think of using this material in the same way we would use a book if we had just taken up playing the guitar for the first time - or any other musical instrument come to that. One step at a time. More will be gained if time is taken to thoroughly investigate each section before progressing on to the next.

We have something of a problem here because we live in a world where most of us move at a rapid pace between one thing and the next. We may find it quite difficult to make ourselves slow down and it may feel quite strange to us. We may never have done anything like this before and it takes discipline not to rush onwards too soon, but this book really does require it and it will be worth the effort.

To help with that process of reflection we suggest the obtaining of a good notebook or the opening of a new file on the computer. (Some journals are available on-line.) In this way it will be possible to make and record some personal on-going responses. The reason for doing this is not to be trendy and arty. It is very practical. We often get things clearer in our heads when we do this sort of thing. We can also look back through the pages and see where we have come from and how our spiritual journey is moving. And keeping a record has a long Catholic tradition behind it. Many of the saints did it and Pope John XXIII gave us an account of his spiritual pilgrimage in his "Journal of a Soul".

There are suggestions in the text about when this might be done.

 ◄ Where you see the Reflect-&-Jot symbol take time to really think through what is said and then get out your notebook or log on. If you like writing that's fine but it might be that you prefer to use diagrams or flow charts or use pictures (your own or from other sources). It doesn't really matter. No one else will see what you do so you can be quite honest - and as messy as you like!

Every chapter has the same format

Symbols:

◀ There's a Way-In section to get us thinking

◀ Inside-The-Text looks at a passage from St John's Gospel, Chapter 21

◀ Digging-Deeper explores what Catholic spirituality says about some themes from the passage

◀ Putting-It-All-Together summarises the main points and highlights what the Church says.

More symbols:

◀ Inside-Out links what we have discovered with how we live our everyday lives.

◀ Pray-A-Psalm ends each chapter but it is important not to think of this as the "prayer bit" of the chapter. The whole section is all designed as a reflective and prayerful process. We have chosen to use the psalms because they are wonderful at expressing so much of what we experience - and Jesus himself used them. We have given some suggestions about how you might make them your own but don't feel bound by these.

◀ There is an extra section entitled All-Together. This gives some ideas about how to share what you have discovered as individuals with others. This could be a group already in existence or gathered especially to look at this topic or just a group of friends meeting over coffee. It is always a good idea to share with others if you can. We have provided ideas about what you could do but you may well need to adapt our suggestions for what to do to the needs of the people in your group. Don't be a slave to our suggested topics!

We hope you will enjoy the book and that it helps you respond to Jesus's question *Do you love me?*

1. Searching

Introduction

Many of us have a head full of unanswered questions to which we would dearly love to know the answers. Some of these are very personal and unique to us; some are questions which human beings have always asked. Many of us also have wish lists, things we would really like to happen; some are mundane and not very important but others are much deeper in us. We all have longings and desires deep in the heart of us but we don't often put them into words. Catholic spirituality says these are very important and, in this chapter, we will be looking at what our spirituality has to say about this inner search for meaning and longing and how it is a part of the spirituality of each one of us.

It is Jesus in fact that you seek when you dream of happiness. He is waiting for you when nothing else you find satisfies you; he is the beauty to which you are so attracted; it is he who provokes you with that thirst for fullness that will not let you settle for compromise.

St John Paul II, 1920-2005

 ◄ Way-In This person is doing what a lot of us do when we get the opportunity; taking a bit of time out. We can't know what thoughts are going on inside as he watches the waves crash on to the shore.

Here are some possibilities:
• Perhaps thinking about the family.
• Perhaps struggling to find answers to why a loved one is ill or had died. Perhaps just feeling a bit lost and wondering where life is going, why he is there at all and what life is all about.
• Perhaps being aware of the wonder of creation and being caught up in it perhaps inside there is a heart full of longing for something or someone that can't quite be put into words - questions about where the longing comes from or why it is there.

Who knows what he is thinking?

 ◄ Reflect-&-Jot If you were standing by this person watching the regular waves beating against the shore what would be your thoughts or questions?

After these things Jesus showed himself again to the disciples by the Sea of Tiberias; and he showed himself in this way. Gathered there together were Simon Peter, Thomas called the Twin, Nathanael of Cana in Galilee, the sons of Zebedee, and two others of his disciples. Simon Peter said to them, *"I am going fishing."* They said to him, *"We will go with you."* They went out and got into the boat, but that night they caught nothing. (*John* 21:1-3)

This is the cause why we are not at rest in heart and soul: that here we seek rest in things that are so little there is no rest in them, and we do not know our God who is all mighty, all wise and all good. For he is true rest

Julian of Norwich, b. 1342

Peter had been through a series of devastating events. Post-traumatic stress is nothing new! We cannot know exactly what was going through his head but we can perhaps imagine it. Jesus, the person he had trusted and loved so much had died a very public, painful and shameful death. It had all happened so quickly and, no doubt Peter's grief was compounded by the fact that he never got to say the things he wanted to say. Why did Jesus have to die? Why did God let it happen? What sort of God is this anyway? And now there's all this talk of the resurrection and those appearances that seemed to be the Jesus he knew of old and yet how could that be? We can't know whether big questions like these were in Peter's head before he gets into the boat but we do know what he does.

Like many of us when grief hits, Peter decides to do something. He gets busy. Life has to go on so he goes back to his old job. There is something very comforting in returning to the familiar routine. So he and his companions go fishing. If Peter thinks he is going to be cheered up by a good return for all his hard labour he is sorely disappointed. It's a disaster. They catch nothing.

◀ Reflect-&-Jot If you were Peter what would you be thinking and feeling?

◀ Digging-Deeper At first sight these verses don't seem to have much to say about spirituality but let's dig a little deeper.

It is you alone whom I desire that I may be where you are, since there is no other joy, no other bliss in heaven or on earth, except in you.

Walter Hilton, 1343-1396

Peter's relationship with Jesus meant that the events of the crucifixion and resurrection were bound to have a huge impact on him. As we shall see Peter was later to realise that all his longings and dreams were to be met in the risen Christ but, as yet, he can't quite sort it out. He's still searching for answers and still longing for the Jesus to whom he has committed his life.

The soul is like an uninhabited world that comes to life only when God lays his head against us.

Thomas Aquinas, 1225-1274

The thirst for someone or something to satisfy our deepest longing lies deep within each of us. It is very deep-seated in us. Catholic spirituality says it is God-given. God has implanted this desire in us. It is a desire for God himself. At the heart of our faith is the knowledge and experience of God's desire for us.

Our spirituality also says that this longing is central to our faith journey because it makes us keep on searching; to travel onwards even if, like Peter, just when we think we have "the answer" God pushes us to experience what that means at a deeper and deeper level.

Christ - the answer

This longing and searching makes us restless but our spirituality says this restlessness is good and holy, God-given and valid. St Augustine (b. 354) summed it up by saying that "our hearts are restless until they rest in God." We see this search expressed in different ways. Some people will put a lot of their energy into going to the gym or football matches. Others will become really involved in building up the local community or in environmental issues. There is nothing wrong in any of these but some are more helpful than others to our spirituality. We need to choose how to respond to our deepest longings (which we will look at later).

> I sought for you abroad
> but you were within me
> though I was far from you.
> Then you touched me, and
> I longed for your peace,
> and now my hope is only
> in your great mercy.
> St Augustine, 354-430

Standing by the Sea of Galilee Peter must have felt really lost that day but, as we shall see, that is exactly where Jesus met him. That's an important insight. Our spirituality says that it is normal to feel lost, to have questions. It is often in our lostness that God meets us because when we are all at sea we are sometimes more open to receive what God has to offer us and to see new paths before us.

> The desire for God is
> written in the human
> heart because we are
> created by God for God.
> *Catechism of the Catholic Church,* 27

 ◀ Reflect-&-Jot It is always good to try and put into words (or if you are a visual person, into picture form) what it is you long for in your heart of hearts.

- When have you felt lost?
- What do you really long for above all else?
- What are you searching for?
- What is it like to know "a restlessness of spirit?"

◀ Inside-Out Peter's response to this situation is to do something.

My Lord God I have no idea where I am going… nor do I really know myself and the fact that I think I am following your will does not mean I am actually doing so. But I believe that my desire to please you does, in fact, please you.

Thomas Merton, 1915-1968

If therefore in the Church everyone does not proceed by the same path, all are called to sanctity and have received an equal privilege of faith through the justice of God.

Vatican II, *Lumen Gentium*, 32

He throws himself into activity. By going fishing he and his companions get on with life as they know it and it is in the middle of that life that things will change. Our spirituality says that living life as we know it is part of our spirituality. It is earthed. This story reminds us that God is found both in the quiet moments where Peter stands on the beach and in the hustle and bustle of our equivalent of fishing. Spirituality is not remote from the way we make decisions, cope with our difficulties, our joys and our grief. The desire to make sense of the life we live and to explore our inner longings is about the whole of us. We find God in both the quiet and in the busyness. Often when we look back over what has happened to us we see that God has been there with us as we have journeyed.

◀ Reflect-&-Jot We find the presence of God in our busyness and in our moments of quiet. Reflect and jot down how you experience this in your own life.

◀ Putting-It-All-Together Catholic spirituality says:

- The thirst for someone or something to satisfy our deepest longing is God-given. Ultimately it is for God.
- Our searching pushes us forward on our spiritual journey and that journey may take many different paths.
- Our restlessness is valid and it is normal to feel lost.
- Spirituality and the ordinary business of living are intertwined. We should not divorce spirituality and life.

◀ Praying-A-Psalm Praying the psalm is more than just reading it slowly. It is reading it with your heart, making it your own prayer. Take some time to slowly pray the psalm. (It is part of psalm 42.) It speaks of the search we are all making and that search is never in vain. If you wish you could select a phrase or a word which stands out for you. Let that stay with you as you go about the rest of the day - or the next day.

As a deer longs for flowing streams
so my soul longs for you, O God.
My soul thirsts for God,
for the living God.
When shall I come and behold
the face of God?

My tears have been my food
day and night,
while people say to me continually,
"Where is your God?"

These things I remember,
as I pour out my soul:
how I went with the throng,
and led them in procession to the house of God,
with glad shouts and songs of thanksgiving,
a multitude keeping festival.

Why are you cast down, O my soul,
and why are you disquieted within me?
Hope in God; for I shall again praise him,
my help and my God.

I say to God, my rock,
"Why have you forgotten me?
Why must I walk about mournfully
because the enemy oppresses me?"

As with a deadly wound in my body,
my adversaries taunt me,
while they say to me continually,
"Where is your God?"

Why are you cast down, O my soul,
and why are you disquieted within me?
Hope in God; for I shall again praise him,
my help and my God.

 ◀ All-Together If you are using this book as part of a group here are some suggestions about what you might do when you come together. Don't try and do them all; do the ones that seem most appropriate to your group.

• Talk about what emerged for you from this chapter, what you found difficult and what energised you. Share as much or as little as you wish from your own reflection.
• Talk about how you found it trying to find time to work with the material in the chapter.
• Share some examples from films, TV or novels where people are expressing their search for meaning.
• If your life were a novel what would be its title and its main story-line?
• How we can help other people express the search for meaning which drives us to develop our spiritualities.

Moving On

Our restless hearts are only satisfied in God. It is exploring the relationship between God and each one of us which lies at the centre of our spirituality, and to which our longings are directed. It is to that we now turn.

2. Recognising

Introduction

In our last chapter we saw how the search for meaning and the fulfilment of our deepest longings and desires is part of our spirituality and leads us forward. In this chapter we shall reflect on the "who" at the centre of all Catholic spirituality and we shall explore something of what being in relationship with that "who" means for each one of us.

For me, prayer is a surge of the heart; it is a simple look turned towards heaven, it is a cry of recognition and of love; embracing both trial and joy.
St Thérèse of Lisieux, 1873-1897

▲ Way-In   Here are three very different pictures. They have nothing in common. We can probably easily recognise what two of them are about although the chances are we will react to them in different ways. For instance the first one may make us think of the silence that happens when it snows or it may remind us of our childhood snowball fights. Some of us may find the middle one joyful because it brings back happy memories. For some it may remind us of something quite painful. The third one is not so obvious. Some people may be bemused by it, others like the colours, others the shape. Some may be challenged by it.

◄ Reflect-&-Jot   Take your time to really look at the pictures and jot down (or draw!) what you recognise in them and what they bring to mind. What attracts you and what confuses you?

Just after daybreak, Jesus stood on the beach; but the disciples did not know that it was Jesus. Jesus said to them, *"Children, you have no fish, have you?"* They answered him, *"No."* He said to them, *"Cast the net to the right side of the boat, and you will find some."* So they cast it, and now they were not able to haul it in because there were so many fish. That disciple whom Jesus loved said to Peter, *"It is the Lord!"* When Simon Peter heard that it was the Lord, he put on some clothes, for he was naked, and jumped into the lake. But the other disciples came in the boat, dragging the net full of fish, for they were not far from the land, only about a hundred yards off. When they had gone ashore, they saw a charcoal fire there, with fish on it, and bread. Jesus said to them, *"Bring some of the fish that you have just caught."* So Simon Peter went aboard and hauled the net ashore, full of large fish, a hundred and fifty-three of them; and though there were so many, the net was not torn. (*John* 21:4-11)

There are three main characters here, Peter, the disciple Jesus loved (usually we call him John) and Jesus himself.

◀ Reflect-&-Jot Read the passage two or three times. What strikes you about it? What do you see in it? It doesn't matter how strange it may seem - jot it down.

◀ Digging-Deeper There is a lot going on in this passage and it has a great deal to say about spirituality.

> The Lord leads all persons by paths and in ways pleasing to him, and each believer responds according to his heart's resolve and the personal expressions of his prayer.
>
> *Catechism of the Catholic Church,* 2699

First and foremost there is Jesus. At first the disciples in the boat don't recognise him at all. He is there but not named. It is often like that for us too. All that happens to us, such as the things we go through, the joys we have and the difficulties we endure, are accompanied by Christ but we often do not recognise his presence. You may be able to think about times when you have looked back and seen how God was with you but you didn't recognise quite how at the time. (Jot it down or find a picture to remind you of it for your journal.)

God takes the initiative

> For a stalk to grow or a flower to open there must be time that cannot be forced; nine months must go by for the birth of a human child; to write a book or compose music often years must be dedicated to patient research... To find the mystery there must be patience, interior purification, silence, waiting.
>
> St John Paul II, 1920-2005

Next we can see from this passage that Jesus sees the disciples before they see him. It is only when he calls out to them that they know he is there. The spirituality of each one of us is a call from the Lord. How do we hear this call? Well, we get a clue from what happens in the account. Jesus takes a gradual approach in order to help the disciples see who he is. If they are wondering about this stranger on the shore and are questioning who he is Jesus doesn't give a direct answer. Instead he asks a question, "have you caught anything?" He then goes on to engage them in both a conversation and a task (put your net over the side). Only then do they recognise him. What Jesus doesn't say is "Hey, look it's me. Get that boat over here and be with me." In other words Jesus takes his time. Our spirituality says that Jesus sees us before we see him and that often we only come to recognise his presence gradually; that the call to grow in relationship with him takes time. Jesus asks us the equivalent of "have you caught anything". He asks, "What's going on for you at the moment?" It is when we take time to reflect and have the equivalent of the conversation which John and Peter had with this stranger that we see who it is before us. It is helpful to know that we should not expect our spiritual journey to bring fulfillment all at once. Consequently we do not need to get discouraged if nothing seems to be happening and we are finding it hard to see where God is.

Recognising

Nevertheless something is happening and in the Gospel we read about that moment of recognition. John is the first to recognise that it is Jesus on the shore. Everything that follows stems from that. At the centre of our spirituality is not a "what to do" or a "how to do it" but a "who". It is a person, the person of Christ. This is a non-negotiable element in our spirituality. If in our prayer and devotions we have not recognised who it is that is before us, we have missed the point. "It is the Lord" says John. John has this flash of recognition, not on his knees in a quiet place but as he is hauling in the net. We can have what we might call recognition moments too. They happen when something occurs, or something is said, or we see something and we just know something special is being shown to us. Our spirituality helps us to see not only what this is but who is there and to respond "It is the Lord". Here is a description of one such moment:

At the heart of catechesis we find, in essence, a Person, the Person of Jesus of Nazareth… It is Jesus who is "the way and the truth and the life," and Christian living consists in following Christ.

St John Paul II, 1920-2005

"I was washing up after breakfast just enjoying that peaceful moment as the house emptied. I don't know what I was thinking but I became aware of a ripple of light through the window as the winter sun popped above the fence. In that moment I knew I was not alone and that God was with me. It was just a moment, but the ordinary joy of that moment, the sense of being loved and accepted, has stayed strong and clear over many long years. It was as if God had said 'Good Morning' just to me."

The next character we meet is Peter. Once John has pointed Jesus out Peter literally leaps into action. He is so anxious to get to Jesus that he throws himself into the sea taking only enough time to grab the essentials. He just can't wait. He doesn't stop to try and get his act together before making for land. Our spirituality says that once we see who this person is there is a real desire to be with him. This is what our hearts have been searching for. Nothing will stop Peter and nothing should stop us; not the awareness of our failures, nor the fact that we have nothing but what God has given us in our hands. It may be fanciful to imagine it but perhaps there was a smile to the face of the risen Lord as he watched the sheer recklessness of Peter's action. For Peter, and for every Christian, nothing else is needed apart from this recognising and being with Christ because everything else stems from it.

I do not have the courage to force myself to search out beautiful prayers in books. There are so many of them it really gives me a head-ache… I say very simply to God what I wish to say. For me prayer is an aspiration of the heart; it is a simple glance directed at heaven, it is a cry of gratitude and love… finally it is something great, supernatural, which expands my soul and unites me to Jesus.

St Thérèse of Lisieux, 1873-1897

25

St Ignatius of Loyola in the sixteenth century summed up this reckless giving of the self to God:

"Take Lord and receive all my liberty, my memory, my understanding, all my will, all I have and possess. You have given all to me, to you Lord, I return it. All is yours, dispose of it wholly according to your will. Give me your love and your grace. With this I am satisfied".

(In your notebook or in your file you might like to re-write this for yourself, using the same ideas but in your own words.)

Keeping the balance

> Prayer is, in my opinion, nothing else than an intimate sharing between friends; it means taking time frequently to be alone with Him who we know loves us.
>
> St Teresa of Avila, 1515-1582

The two disciples, Peter and John, balance each other. John has a pivital role to play because he is the first to recognise who this person standing on the shore is. Peter does more than look. Once John has pointed Jesus out to him Peter acts - he jumps into the sea and makes his way towards Jesus. John and Peter are like two sides of one coin. John recognises and then Peter turns the recognition into action. Our spirituality says we need both. It is not enough for us to see "It is the Lord" we also have to "jump into the sea" and trust in the relationship into which we have been called. Spirituality is all about making that journey towards the Lord we have recognised.

Finally, Jesus makes himself known to these two together. Spirituality is not a purely personal and private thing, though it is that too. As we shall see, we make this spiritual journey on our own and in the company of others. Peter needs John to help him see the Lord, John needs Peter to help put the recognition into action.

▼ Reflect-&-Jot Here are some pictures of Jesus. You will probably like some more than others. Take your time to look at them.

- What is it you see in the pictures? In other words what might each one tell you about who Jesus is for you?
- Recall a time when, looking back now, you can recognise the presence of Christ with you - even if you didn't see him at the time.
- Who has been John for you - helping you to recognise the Lord?
- Who has been Peter for you - helping you to put your prayer into action?

◀ Inside-Out Recognising the Lord and making our way towards him, which is at the centre of our spirituality, is no easy task. Jesus calls us and accompanies us every step of the way and he has given us some treasures to help us on the journey. Jesus talked about a wise person knowing how to bring out from the treasury things old and new. (*Matthew* 13:52)

> Private prayer is like straw scattered here and there; if you set it on fire it makes a lot of little flames. But gather these straws into a bundle and light them and you get a mighty fire, rising like a column into the sky; public prayer is like that.
>
> St John Baptist Vianney, 1786-1859

We have already seen one of these treasures: Peter and John come to the Lord together. Spirituality might be individual but it is never individualistic. So, one of our treasures is the practice of praying together. As we pray with one another we discover that in some special way God is in our midst. That may mean an intimate sharing of prayer with one other person, or it may take the form of a group saying the Rosary, or going to a Taizé evening, or a contemplative prayer group. There are lots of different ways.

It is important also to remember that these and many other forms of praying together are not in competition with the liturgical rites of the Church. It is not a case of either/or but of both. What is important is to take on board that sharing with others in the liturgy enriches other forms of prayer, both personal and communal. And similarly they deepen our experience of liturgy which is the source and summit of our Christian life.

> Father I am seeking, I am hesitant and uncertain, but will you, O God, watch over each step of mine and guide me.
>
> St Augustine, 354-430

Another of these treasures is that of *pilgrimage*. It might be to a well known pilgrimage place like Lourdes or Jerusalem or it might be much more local. There is something about walking and talking, praying and sharing food together which is very special. Times of laughter and times of silence together help us to see and encounter the God who walks with us.

There is another treasure related to the friends we have here who accompany us as we see and respond to God. Catholic spirituality has a profound understanding of the *communion of saints*. Pre-eminent among these is Our Lady. Countless Catholics have found in her a way to be present to God and an example to follow. She, above all, had her Son as her focus and her "yes" to God is the supreme example of recognising the call of God and responding. In addition, thousands of women and men, some named by the Church, some unnamed, have gone before us. Their lives have shone out as beacons to the truth that Christ is risen and life finds it's meaning in him. They have all had Christ at the centre of their spirituality.

nd it was that relationship which enabled them to live, and ften to die, as they did. Some found their spirituality leading hem into lives of service for others; some into lives of deep rayer for the church and the world; some into challenging he structures of power. All of them had the same focus. Like ohn they recognised the Lord and like Peter they responded n all their different ways. For all of them the non-negotiable lement was the person of Christ and what he meant to them. Ve ask Mary and all the saints to pray for us just as we ask for he prayers of those we know here on earth.

St Gianna Beretta Molla

Our spirituality is never self-indulgent and a wise person vill know that there is much merit in seeing how others ecognise and come to the Lord. God uses other people to ead us along and God uses us to help them. Sometimes it is jood to have one particular person with whom we share the tory of our relationship with God. Such a person can listen o us. As we verbalise things, we often hear ourselves telling ur story and recognise, as if for the first time, what God is loing within us. A person like this can affirm and encourage s. Such a companion is not there to tell us where to go, she r he simply walks alongside us. It's like having someone look it the map of our own walk with God and assuring us that he road ahead is safe. Other people always help us to keep a jalance within ourselves.

There are many other treasures in our spiritual storehouse nd we will look at some others in our next chapter.

◄ Reflect-&-Jot Reflect on the experiences of praying with others which you have had. Put down whatever comes to mind for you.

- Which of the saints is especially important to you? Why?
- How do you think they help you see and respond to God?
- When have the prayers of others meant a lot to you?
- What did they mean for you?

◀ Putting-It-All-Together Catholic spirituality says:

- Christ accompanies us but we don't always recognise him. He is the stranger on the shore.
- Christ sees us before we see him and calls us to our own unique spiritual path.
- We often come to the point of recognition ("It is the Lord") gradually; the call to grow in relationship takes time.
- The centre of our spirituality is a who - the person of Christ. We are called to recognise him (like John) and respond (like Peter).
- The desire to be in relationship with God, in Christ, lies at the heart of our spirituality because everything else springs from it.
- Our spiritual path is made in the company of others, here on earth and in heaven.

◀ Pray-A-Psalm Pray the psalm with your heart, making it your own prayer. (It is part of psalm 139.) It speaks of God knowing us through and through and that there is nowhere we can go where God cannot be met, recognised and known. If you wish you might like to read it out loud prayerfully two or three times putting different emphasis on different words each time. Then take time to savour them and hear what God is saying to you.

O Lord you have searched me and known me.
You know when I sit down and when I rise up;
you discern my thoughts from far away.

You search out my path and my lying down,
and are acquainted with all my ways.
Even before a word is on my tongue,
O Lord, you know it completely.

You hem me in, behind and before,
and lay your hand upon me.
Such knowledge is too wonderful for me;
it is so high I cannot attain it.

Where can I go from your spirit?
Or where can I flee from your presence?
If I ascend to heaven, you are there;
if I make my bed in Sheol, you are there.

If I take the wings of the morning
and settle at the farthest limits of the sea,
even there your hand shall lead me,
and your right hand shall hold me fast.

If I say "Surely darkness shall cover me,
and the light around me become night",
even the darkness is not dark to you;
the night is as bright as the day,
for darkness is as light to you.

For it was you who formed my inward parts;
you knit me together in my mother's womb.
I praise you for I am fearfully and wonderfully made.
Wonderful are your works, that I know very well.

My frame was not hidden from you,
when I was being made in secret,
intricately woven in the depths of the earth.
Your eyes beheld my unformed substance.

In your book were written
all the days that were formed for me,
when none of them as yet existed.
How weighty to me are your thoughts, O God!
How vast the sum of them!
I try to count them - they are more than the sand;
I come to an end - I am still with you.

◀ All-Together If you are using this book as part of a group here are some suggestions about what you might do when you come together. Don't try and do them all; some of them might not be appropriate for your group.

- Talk about one thing which emerged for you from this chapter. Share as much or as little as you wish from your own reflection.
- Pass an egg-timer (the sort that has sand in it) around the circle and each person has the time it takes for the sand to run out to say what they felt it would be like to be Peter when John says "It is the Lord". No interrupting or discussion allowed until everyone who wishes has spoken.
- How can we be John for others, helping them to recognise "It is the Lord"?
- Pray the psalm together - perhaps a paragraph each round the group.
- Ask everyone to write down their name on a piece of paper and put them in a hat (or whatever). Mix them up. Each person takes one. Pray for that person this week. If you pick your own name put it back and get another!

Moving On

We have seen how at the centre of our spirituality is a relationship. We have begun to see some of the treasures we have which help us to recognise the Christ who is with us and to respond. What it means to grow in that friendship and the treasures which help us to do that is the theme of our next chapter.

3. Experiencing

In the previous chapter we saw that at the centre of our spirituality is the person of Christ and we also thought about the importance of recognising him and responding. We also explored some of the treasures we have in our tradition that help us do that. Like all relationships, we experience coming to know Jesus in different ways and in this chapter we shall explore different aspects of what that can mean for us.

◀ Way-In Here are some pictures which highlight some of the different ways in which we communicate with one another.

Christ Jesus…is present in many ways to his Church: in his word, in his Church's prayer, "where two or three are gathered in my name", in the poor, the sick and the imprisoned, in the sacraments of which he is the author, in the sacrifice of the Mass…but "he is present…most especially in the Eucharistic species".
Catechism of the Catholic Church,
1373

We come to know other people through conversing with them. We will think a little more deeply about this way of communicating in our next chapter. We also grow in our friendships in other ways and experience their love through observation, how they act in different situations, through their body language, through touch and through just being with them in companionable silence. Not all communication is obvious. People can get to know each other in all sorts of different ways.

◀ Reflect-&-Jot Take time to think about a significant relationship in your own life. Jot down the many ways you got to know the other person and what helped that relationship to grow.

When they had gone ashore, they saw a charcoal fire there, with fish on it, and bread. Jesus said to them, *"Bring some of the fish that you have just caught."* So Simon Peter went aboard and hauled the net ashore, full of large fish, a hundred and fifty-three of them; and though there were so many, the net was not torn. Jesus said to them, *"Come and have breakfast."* Now none of the disciples dared to ask him, *"Who are you?"* because they knew it was the Lord. Jesus came and took the bread and gave it to them, and did the same with the fish. This was now the third time that Jesus appeared to the disciples after he was raised from the dead. *(John* 21:9-14)

We have no idea what went on between Peter and Jesus when Peter gets to the beach before the others. When, however, the boat is dragged up the beach we find, not some great moment of revelation like the Transfiguration, but a humble picnic. There is a fire, something to eat and company. It is in this setting that Jesus communicates with his friends and he does it in several ways.

◀ Reflect-&-Jot Read the Gospel passage again. Try and picture the scene. If you were there where would you be - who would you be? What would you say? If you like, write the conversation down or sketch yourself in the scene or choose some pictures which would express how you might react to the invitation.

◀ Digging-Deeper This short Gospel passage is packed with images about how our spirituality helps us to experience the reality of the Lord with us. Let's look at them one at a time and see how they apply to us.

God in the Ordinary

First this whole scene happens in a familiar place with familiar people with familiar things. There's the beach they know, the friends they know, and a simple meal they would have eaten many times before. But amid these ordinary things an extra-ordinary meeting happens. This is a privileged moment for the disciples. We have such privileged moments too. We quite rightly talk about the sacraments as special moments, special encounters with the Lord, which they are. But our sacramental life occurs in a world in which God is already present. Just as these disciples experienced him in the middle of their ordinary daily business, for us too God uses the ordinary, the familiar, the commonplace as ways through which to communicate and meet us. We will look at those particular moments we call sacraments later but, for now, it is good to realise that the whole world can be sacramental; a meeting place with the risen Lord. Our spirituality says that God comes to us and our relationship with God is developed in the midst of the ordinary.

Gifts

The image of the charcoal fire has it's own significance. Jesus has lit a fire for a very pragmatic reason - in order to cook breakfast. He has even provided the food, some fish is already cooking on it. But Jesus also asks the disciples to bring some of the fish they have caught. Our spirituality says that God does both for us. God certainly provides for us and offers to us what is best for us but God also asks us to bring our own gifts. We do this ritually at every Mass during the Offertory. Throughout our lives, however, God works with and through the gifts of our own personality and talents and dispositions to help us grow in our spiritual life. We are all different and because of this we all pray differently. These different ways are God's gift to us and so it is good to pray as the persons we are and in the particular ways God has given to us.

Breathing spaces

Jesus has also lit this fire to provide the disciples with much needed refreshment and rest. Physically they have been fishing all night. No doubt they were very hungry and tired and Jesus responds to this very human need. We shouldn't read too much into the text but perhaps Jesus also lit it to reassure the disciples. It has all been too much and what they need is some recharging. In order to live a balanced life we do need to have breathing spaces. These provide us with the opportunity to see things from a different angle or make deeper connections. Our spirituality says times of rest and refreshment are important. They are part of our spiritual treasury. In the Scriptures the Sabbath image offers us the idea of a regular stopping time and, in the history of the Church, we can see how this balance of stopping and then doing shines through in the life of many of our religious orders with their history of getting a proper balance between praying, doing and resting.

Take & Eat

Next we hear an invitation, "Come and have breakfast". And here we hear echoes of that other meal where Jesus says "Take, eat". This fish, which the disciples have brought from their own everyday life, is to be the means through which they are fed. In this passage we see a small community (the disciples), the risen Lord and the meal; the same components that we find in every Mass today. This picnic on the beach is not a Eucharist as such but it is an image of what Catholic spirituality has always, believed, known and experienced, namely that at the Eucharist, the followers of Jesus gather with each other around the altar and are fed with the Lord himself. He is the bread of life, the food of travellers, the lamb who sacrificed himself to take away our sins.

Silence

The next thing that happens is unspoken. The disciples know "it is the Lord" and, at the same time, they want to know who he is! It seems paradoxical. If they know why do they need to ask? And yet there is an insight here. Sometimes as we grow in our relationship with Jesus we know something deep down but at the same time, can't quite make sense of it. It is then, like the disciples, that we need to leave it unspoken. One of the great treasures in our spirituality is the experience of silence. We live in a very noisy and sound-ridden world. We are wired for sound with our mobile phones, iPods, and computers. Sometimes we are so unused to silence that, faced with it, we would prefer to fill it up with noise. And when we do find it, we can sometimes be unsure what to do with it. Yet our spirituality says silence is important. It values silence because silence helps us hear where God is calling us to a more balanced life. The great Trappist monk, Thomas Merton once said, "We are what we do with our silence".

◀ Reflect-&-Jot Look at each of the paragraphs above and underline the things which • reassure you • surprise you • challenge you. Put them in your notebook or on your computer - using your own words if you can.

◀ Inside-Out Everything we have seen so far is about the means the Lord gives us to grow in relationship with him. Exactly how we do this and how we use the treasures we have been given will be different for each one of us but there are plenty of opportunities to choose from. Let's look at each of the major images we have outlined above and see the different practical ways we can make them our own. To do this we will have a "Try-One-Of-These" section after each paragraph so that we can put the theory into action.

God in the ordinary

Do you wish to honour the Body of Christ? Then do not disdain him when you see him in rags. After having honoured him in church do not leave him to die of cold outside for lack of clothing.

St John Chrysostom, 347-407

First we talked about God using the ordinary to communicate with us. Everything has the potential to speak to us of God, even our failures. It is not just the big things like the birth of a child or the loss of a loved one, it is also in the smaller everyday things of life; the smile someone gives us when we are feeling really down, the laughter we share with a friend, the look on the face of a homeless person. If we make a conscious effort to keep our eyes open we will find God everywhere, drawing us on, conversing with us through others, challenging us through the injustices we see.

Try-One-Of-These

- Look out for where God is with you today. Keep asking yourself "Was that God I just saw and heard?"
- Tomorrow evening spend a while looking back on the day and asking yourself "Where have I experienced God?"

Gifts

It is by the path of love, which is charity, that God draws near to mankind, and mankind to God. But where love is not found, God cannot dwell. If then, we possess love, we possess God.

St Albert the Great, 1206-1280

Next we looked at how God works with our own personalities and the gifts we bring. God asks us to "bring some of the fish" that is ourselves, and our spirituality needs to take this into account. We come to God as we are with all our foibles and quirkiness and that is the person God loves. It is the "who I am" that God works with. God does not wait for us to reach some level of perfection before we can experience what it means to be in that relationship of love. It is true that part of our spirituality is about being open enough to allow God to get rid of those parts of us that are not in line with the wholeness God wants for us. But that is a very different hing to changing our personalities. We are who we are so we have to walk a balance between knowing what God wishes us to change and what God wishes us to treasure. And there is a lot we should treasure.

This huge range of difference between us means that different people will prefer different ways of praying. Some people need a lot of quiet, others like to sing. Some like to pray with words, others with pictures or symbols. Some like to pray using the same phrases over and over (like the Rosary), others prefer quiet meditation on one word or none at all. Some like to dance, some like to kneel. There is no one method. It is important that we pray as we can, and that we don't try to pray in ways that simply don't suit us. We need to find what is right for us, our personalities and the situations in which we find ourselves.

Try-One-Of-These

• If you were to write your own obituary what would you say?
• What would you be remembered for? What makes you, you?
• When you pray do you prefer prayer with a lot of quiet "being" in it or do you prefer to pray in ways that engage your mind a lot? Pray that way and thank God for the gift of your own particular way of prayer.
• Do you have a favourite prayer? If so why is it special to you? Write it out in your journal if you wish.
• Could you try praying in a different way? You could choose from some of those mentioned above.

Breathing Spaces

The third area we looked at was to do with our need for breathing spaces if we are to live a balanced life. Times of rest and refreshment are important if we are to deepen our experience of the Lord. If you are lucky you may be able to make regular space in your life. Some people go away for a day every so often or on retreat once a year. If you can, that is great but not everyone can do that. If it is simply not possible to get away that doesn't mean it is not possible to take time out. There are other ways. We can create small breathing spaces in everyday life. Waiting for the kettle to boil, standing at the bus stop, sitting on the train or walking the dog. Having a "cup of tea with God" in your favourite armchair or digging the garden. They all have potential to be

The great method of prayer is to have none. If in going to prayer one can form in oneself a pure space for receiving the Spirit of God, that will suffice all method.
St Jane Frances de Chantal, 1572-1641

little spaces of refreshment which allow God to get through to us. One real opportunity is at the end of the day when we get the chance to look back and see what has happened. What has given us energy that day and spoken to us of God with us and what has sapped the energy and prevented us from conversing with the God of our life?

Try-One-Of-These

- Pick one of the ideas from the suggestions above and give it a go. If it works that's great. If not, it doesn't mean you are a failure. It simply means this is just not for you at this time. Try something else.

- Create a prayer space at home. You could use a candle and an open Bible as your focus, or a crucifix or a picture or whatever helps you to see this space as special. It doesn't need to be there permanently, just for the time you are there!

Take, Eat

Holy Communion augments our union with Christ. The principal fruit of receiving the Eucharist in Holy Communion is an intimate union with Christ Jesus... Life in Christ has its foundation in the Eucharistic banquet.

Catechism of the Catholic Church, 1391

Our fourth area was about being fed and nourished. We heard Jesus's invitation to "come and have breakfast" and we linked this to the Eucharist. For some people going to Mass has become something of a routine, for others it's a bore, for others it is a fantastic experience of encounter. The truth is that the Lord is always there regardless of our disposition. The One who is before us never changes. It is also true that we need to eat whether we feel like it or not. If we don't get some nourishment from somewhere we literally fade away. So whatever we feel like at the time, it is important that we respond to the invitation of Jesus to "take, eat".

As far as possible, you should pray in quiet and silent devotion. Try to have a favourite topic of prayer, such as devotion to the passion of Christ, the Blessed Sacrament... go directly to Jesus without too much fuss.

St Peter Eymard, 1868-1962

Nevertheless our *response* to what is offered to us in the Eucharist is profoundly affected by the spirit in which we come. If we come seeing this as a true meeting with the Lord with whom we are in relationship and whom we long to know more deeply, that will make all the difference. Even when we really don't feel much is going on, our spirituality tells us that here the Lord comes, not just to meet us, but to live in us. Even if we feel nothing at all that is the reality. It is he who feeds us with his own self as we make our pilgrimage towards what we are called to become. Just as that picnic on the beach was a privileged moment for the disciples so all our sacraments are special moments in which the Lord, who is always present to us everywhere comes in a particular way.

Try-One-Of-These

- Express on paper what the Eucharist means to you. You could make a list of words or a diagram or find a picture.
- Try to recall what God is about to do as you walk or drive to church. Alternatively you could get there a bit earlier.
- What prayer will be in your heart as you attend Mass next time? Write it down.
- The word Eucharist means thanksgiving so recall the times you have been fed by God in the past and give thanks.

Silence

The section above looked at the importance of silence in our spirituality. Real silence though is not just an absence of noise. We can be very noisy indeed on the inside even if the outside is quiet. It is also possible to be quiet on the inside while chaos reigns on the outside. This is because, as we have seen, silence helps us get in touch with our real selves and opens the path for us to hear the still, small voice of God. Silence is indeed golden. For some of us, however, befriending silence is not easy. It can be difficult to find some silence in a noisy world, especially as it is such a rarity. It can be difficult because we are not used to it and we so easily get distracted. Sometimes we forget that the mind is there to think with. It abhors a vacuum so it is well nigh impossible for it to stop thinking. But we can quieten it and the worst thing we can do with distractions is be distracted by them. Let them go. Do not beat yourself up about them or give them undue attention. What silence does is to help us shift to a different interior space. It opens us up and balances us. So, how can we befriend it and discover the immense value it has?

I ask you to look into your hearts each day, to find the source of all true love. Jesus is always there... Deep within your heart he is calling you to spend time with him in prayer, but this kind of prayer, real prayer, requires discipline... Even amidst the stress and business of our daily lives we need to make space for silence because it is in silence that we find God, and in silence that we discover our true self.

Benedict XVI

Try-One-Of-These

- If you are happy with silence try jotting down exactly why it helps you in your spiritual life.
- Try spending a short time (say five minutes) in quiet every day. Do not worry if nothing much seems to be happening!
- If you are easily distracted in times of quiet have a piece of paper and pen beside you and make a note of what your distractions are. Once you have them on paper you might find it easier to put them to one side or you might find that God is saying something to you through them.
- Choose your favourite name for God (Father, Abba, Lord, or the name of Jesus) and if your mind wanders in the quiet bring it back by repeating the word in your head.
- Concentrate on your breathing. Don't try and change it but think of yourself breathing in the life of God and breathing out whatever is bothering you.

 ◄ Reflect-&-Jot As you try out some of the above, for each one jot down in your notebook or file how you reacted.

 ◄ Putting-It-All-Together Catholic spirituality says:

- God uses the ordinary, the familiar, the commonplace as ways to meet us.
- God works with the gifts of our own personality and dispositions. We experience what it means to be in relationship with the Lord by praying in the way that is right for us.
- In order to live a balanced life we need to have breathing spaces.
- In the Eucharist we are fed and so grow in our relationship with God.
- One of the greatest treasures we have is the gift of silence.

◀ Pray-A-Psalm Take some time to slowly pray the psalm. (It is psalm 131.) It gives us the image of a relationship of trust, of a fed child, quietly resting in hope. Reflect on what message it gives of the relationship between God and you. Pray about it.

O Lord my heart is not lifted up,
my eyes are not raised too high;
I do not occupy myself with things
too great and too marvellous for me.
But have calmed and quieted my soul,
like a weaned child with its mother;
my soul within me is like a weaned child.

O Israel hope in the Lord
From this time on and for evermore.

 ◀ All-Together If you are using this book as part of a group here are some suggestions about how to share reflections on the contents of this chapter and what you might have discovered from it. Pick and choose what suits your group.

- Share stories about how you have discovered God communicating with you in the ordinary events of life.
- Share what forms of prayer suit you best and bring you closer to God.
- What could you as a group do to provide others with a breathing space in your parish?
- Could you, would you, like to arrange an event where people could experience some silence. If so, what might this be and what is the next step?
- What do you find difficult about silence? What do you find helpful about it?
- Pass a lit candle round the group. Each person holds it for a short time and prays in silence for whatever they wish. Other members of the group pray for that person in silence.

Moving On

We have explored a lot of ways in which we can open ourselves more fully to God. We experience the presence of God in the world in which we live, through the sacraments, through making space and through silence. We also do it by entering into a conversation with the Lord. It is to that conversation that we turn next.

4. Conversing

Introduction

We all know what it is like when our communication with another person breaks down and how uncomfortable that makes us feel. We also know what it is like to have a really good conversation with someone; the sort of conversation where we are so deeply engrossed that time flies. Sometimes we come away from such conversations knowing that the encounter has changed the way we think about things or knowing that in some way we have been deeply enriched.

Through his Word, God speaks to man. By words, mental or vocal, our prayer takes flesh. Yet it is most important that the heart should be present to him to whom we are speaking in prayer....

Catechism of the Catholic Church, 2700

 ◀ Way-In Here are some pictures of people in conversation with each other.

◀ Reflect-&-Jot Jot down what these pictures say to you about what makes for good conversation?

Take time to think about a significant conversation you have had. You might like to find a photo, if you have one, of the person with whom you had the conversation and put it in your journal to remind you of it. Make a few notes about why the conversation was so important to you?

◂ Inside-The-Text When we left the risen Lord meeting the disciples on the beach, they were all eating breakfast. Here is what happens next.

When they had finished breakfast, Jesus said to Simon Peter, *"Simon, son of John, do you love me more than these?"* He said to him, *"Yes, Lord; you know that I love you."* Jesus said to him, *"Feed my lambs."* A second time he said to him, *"Simon, son of John, do you love me?"* He said to him, *"Yes, Lord; you know that I love you."* Jesus said to him, *"Tend my sheep."* He said to him the third time, *"Simon, son of John, do you love me?"* Peter felt hurt because he said to him the third time, *"Do you love me?"* And he said to him, *"Lord, you know everything; you know that I love you."* Jesus said to him, *"Feed my sheep."* (*John 21:15-17*)

This passage gives us an account of the intimate conversation between Jesus and Peter. It was a conversation which it is unlikely Peter ever forgot.

 ◄ Reflect-&-Jot What do you notice about this conversation?

 ◄ Digging-Deeper We have already seen that Catholic spirituality is centred on a relationship with Christ. As we have seen in the previous chapter the relationship with God grows and develops in all sorts of ways and this can happen through the many and various opportunities that come our way. However, throughout the centuries our spirituality explores what it means for the Christian to be in dialogue with the Lord; having a conversation. When people talk about prayer this is often what they mean.

Prayer – A Genuine Conversation

To begin with it is worth noting that it is Jesus who initiates this conversation and he does it by using Peter's original name. "Simon, son of John". Names are more significant than we often realise. Our name is intimately connected to our identity, which is why we often get upset if it is misused or abused. Some of us are called one name by acquaintances and another by our closest family and friends. We don't like it if people who don't really know us use our most familiar name; that is usually reserved for the people who know us really well; those with whom we have some sort of relationship. Jesus calls us by that familiar name because our relationship with him is unique and intimate. He does the same with Peter, he calls him by the name he was given at birth, Simon.

Prayer ought to be fervent, resigned, persevering, and accompanied with great reverence. One should consider that he stands in the presence of God and speaks with a Lord before whom all the angels tremble from awe and fear.
St Mary Magdalen de Pazzi, 1556-1607

Next we see that this is conversation as we usually think of it; two people in dialogue, speaking and listening. Having made it clear that this is a conversation solely with Simon, son of John, and no one else, Jesus begins with a very direct question. There is no beating about the bush here. Jesus digs deep, "Do you love me?" Peter responds immediately, not by using the name he knows so well (Jesus) but by using the title, Lord. This shows us that Peter is acutely aware that this relationship is not one of equals. This is important for us too. I am not equal with Jesus. Of course he is the Jesus who walked the roads and laughed and cried as we do. He is the Jesus who knows from experience what it is to be human but he is far more that that. So our conversation, like Peter's, is with the Lord Jesus. Jesus of Nazareth and Lord. This is not the place to delve deeply into the theology of the person of Christ and his relationship to the Father and the Spirit but a little thought here can help us in our prayer and save us from some pitfalls.

Prayer - Conversing With the Real Jesus

Some people see Jesus as little more than a good man, or an example for us to follow, or even a good man raised from the dead. But the Church says he is far more than that. Other people see Jesus as "God dressed up as a human being", who, because he is God, cannot be aware of what it is really like to be human, but the Church says that is not right either. Jesus is both truly human and truly divine. He is not one more than the other. He is God and man.

It may be hard to understand this but we need to be able to grasp such truth because it affects how our conversation goes. So, for instance, there may be times when something has happened to us and we are only too aware of the glory and wonder of God. Then we are right to have the sort of conversation that recognises and celebrates that. At those times our conversation may well focus on the risen and ascended Lord of all creation. At other times something may have occurred which plunges us into the dark places of human frailty. We are overcome with grief or pain or remorse or hurt and then our conversation is with the Jesus who is my brother and friend, to whom I can say anything and to whom I pour out my heart, Jesus of Nazareth. We need both. Getting this balance is good because it stops our conversation with the risen Lord being either so heavenly minded it is no earthly use or so earthly that we miss out on the wonder of the fact that we are in dialogue with the holy.

> We must speak to God as a friend speaks to his friend, servant to his master; now asking some favour, now acknowledging our faults, and communicating to Him all that concerns us, our thoughts, our fears, our projects, our desires, and in all things seeking his counsel.
> St Ignatius of Loyola, 1491-1556

Prayer - A Continuing Conversation

The conversation between Peter and the Lord continues. Peter responds to the question Jesus asked. He affirms his love for Christ with the words, "Yes Lord, you know that I love you." This is not a wishy-washy expression of feeling. In fact it has little to do with feelings at all. Peter is saying yes to Christ, knowing that in the past he had said no. Just as he had three times denied Jesus so this conversation, which contains three questions, restores him. Now he has the chance to affirm his commitment. So Jesus repeats his

"Tell Me about everything and know that this will give Me great joy." I answered "But you know about everything Lord." And Jesus replied to me, "Yes, I do know but you should not excuse yourself with the fact that I know, but with childlike faith talk to me about everything for my ears and heart are inclined towards you."

St Faustina, 1905-1938

question twice more. "Simon, son of John do you love me?" And each time Peter responds. Now this conversation back and forth between Jesus and Peter can suggest three things to us.

It suggests that our conversations with the Lord are not so much about receiving nice comfy feelings as about saying "yes" to a relationship which will challenge us as much as it will comfort us, and stretch us as much as it will embrace us. It will affect who we are and what we do. It also suggests that sometimes God has to ask us the same questions over and over again as he did with Peter. Here is how one person describes it.

"I had this niggling idea in my head. It was as if Christ was asking me "Well Ben, what are you going to do about Sarah?" Being me, I hoped the situation would resolve itself so that I wouldn't have to do anything. But it kept coming back. "What are you going to do about Sarah?" In the end I knew I just had to stop procrastinating and raise the issue with her about how long, at her age, she could go on living on her own and whether or not she should come and live with us."

That experience is a record of a conversation not a million miles away from the one Peter had. The Lord was asking Ben a question and Ben was responding, even if reluctantly and after several prompts.

Thirdly it suggests that sometimes this conversation may not be easy. Peter felt hurt because of the questions Jesus asked. Was he hurt because they were a painful reminder of how he had denied Jesus three times and run away? Or was he hurt because Jesus did not seem to believe him when he avowed his love? Conversations are easily misunderstood and it is important to try and ensure our dialogue with the Lord does not become a way of hearing what we want to hear or a way of opting out from responding to whatever we are being called to. We'll see how we can guard against this later.

Finally this passage gives us one further clue about what might happen in our own conversations with the Lord. After each one of the responses given by Peter, Jesus issues a command. This is what you are to *do*. Peter is well and truly given his orders - feed my sheep. It is right and proper that we spend time in quiet conversation with the Lord simply listening and speaking. We must also realise that almost ertainly we will be led to do something. Prayer and living he Christian life are intricately bound to each other. To know hrist and to profess to love him inevitably lead to sharing is mission of love for others as well, to feed his sheep in whatever way we are called to do so. We'll look at that a little more in our next chapter.

So how can we engage in this sort of conversation? How do we do it? Before we look at that let's just reflect.

◀ Reflect-&-Jot In your journal, or on your computer, record a time (if you can think of one) when you knew that God had something to say to you.

What makes conversation with the Lord difficult or problematic or, at the moment, impossible for you? Is there something that gets in the way? Be honest and record it in some way.
• What ONE thing would you want to say most? Say it in your journal in whatever way you wish (words, poems, photos etc).
• God calls us by name. Let yourself be called by your name. You might want to write out your name in some way in your journal.

◀ Inside-Out

Developing the conversation - first things first

So how do we go about developing this conversation? The first thing we need to do is to think about *who* we are talking to. If we are going to invest time and energy in developing a conversation we do well to sort out to whom we are talking and listening. This passage is about one person having a conversation with Jesus. We may be tempted to think it was alright for Peter, after all he did have Jesus in front of him. But what about us? Some of us may even be thinking that our prayer, our conversation, is seldom with Jesus at all. We think and pray using other words to communicate with God. Perhaps we think more about God as Father. Some of us are happier imaging our relationship with God like this and naturally call God Father. Others of us have unhappy or painful memories about fatherhood and we naturally gravitate to conversing with Jesus the Lord so our prayers are addressed more to the Lord Jesus. Still

A prayer in which a person is not aware of whom he is speaking to, what he is asking, who it is who is asking and of whom, I don't call prayer...however much the lips may move.
St Teresa of Avila, 1515-1582

others develop a strong and intimate relationship with th
Holy Spirit. For others their prayer begins with Mary an
through her to God. All true Christian prayer is made to Go
who is one, Father, Son and Spirit. However we address Go
what is pointed out to us in this passage is still important.

Try-One-Of-These (or more if you wish!)

• Before you begin your conversation spend a while just thinking about both the wonder of who you are about to address. Then open the conversation using the name of Jesus, the name Joseph and Mary gave him.
• Jesus said that he and the Father are one (*John* 14:11). He used the familiar name any child used for her or his father, "Abba". We can use it too (*Romans* 8:15). Before conversing with God try repeating that name quietly and slowly in your head for a few moments. Take your time.
• Think of a time when something wonderful happened to you, when something moved you deeply. Open your conversation with words of thanks to the Lord of all.

Jot down what happened in your journal.

Developing the conversation - where and when we converse

It is possible to offer fervent prayer even while working in public, or strolling alone, or seated in your shop... while buying or selling or even while cooking.
St John Chrysostom, 347-407

Peter had his dialogue with the Lord on the beach, a place he knew well. It was his place of work. As we know from ex-perience our conversations with people happen in all sorts of contexts and situations. The same is true of our dialogue with God. It can be anywhere and at any time. As we have seen finding a specific time and space is important but that does not mean our prayer is limited to that. It is possible and we can engage in this conversation in the middle of a very busy life.

Try-This

Make a conscious effort in the next twenty-four hours to speak and listen to God on two or three occasions during the day whatever you are doing. Use your own words to say something to God about what is happening to you or others or how you are affected by something that is going on. Remember to listen too.

Jot down what happened in your journal.

Developing the conversation - making use of the treasure of Scripture

As we have already explored, God becomes known to us in many ways. However, we have also been given some treasures which God uses to converse with us. One of the most important of these is Scripture. One of the documents of the Second Vatican Council puts it beautifully when it states "In the Scriptures, the Father, who is in heaven, comes lovingly to his children and speaks with them." (Dei Verbum, 21)

Throughout the centuries the Church has discovered that reflecting on, and responding to, the words of Scripture is a primary way of conversing with God. We talk about it as the Word of God, and words are central to conversation. The trouble is that for many of us opening up this treasure has either never happened or has proved difficult.

> Prayer should accompany the reading of sacred Scripture, so that it becomes a dialogue between God and the human reader.
> Vatican II, *Dei Verbum*, 25

> We speak to God when we pray, we listen to Him when we read the divine oracles.
> St Ambrose, circa 334-394

Try-One-Of-These

• Find a quiet space. Take a Gospel passage and read it slowly and prayerfully. Then read it a second time. What one word or phrase stands out for you? Speak to God about it and listen to what that word is saying to you. You can, of course converse with God this way using any piece of Scripture.

• Read the account of the leper whom Jesus heals. (*Luke* 5:12-16) Read it slowly twice, then put the passage aside and try and imagine yourself in the scene. You may be the leper or one of the crowd or an unnamed observer. Let yourself become part of the action. What does God say to you? When this comes to a natural end speak to God about it.

• Take a psalm (try psalm 130) and after reading it prayerfully re-write it in your own words. Take your time and allow your re-writing to be your words to God. Remember to listen to what God is saying to you as the words come. Put it in your journal.

• Take a phrase from the Scriptures in which God is speaking in the first person, (e.g. I am the Lord your healer, or I am the light of the world, or You are precious in my eyes and I love you). Spend some time letting God say these words to you then use them as your prayer for other people. You might like to name the persons followed by the phrase.

Jot down what happened in your journal or file.

We have other riches in our treasury too which can help u in our conversation with the Lord. We have ancient prayer. which have been handed down to us which we can make ou own. We have hymns old and new and a whole host of poetry and prose. We can draw on all of these to express our response to God and to listen to what the Lord has to say.

We also have resources in the wider world, music in all it: forms, art, dance, the natural world, stories and literature and much more can all be used to express what we want to say to God and the means God uses to converse with us.

Try-One-Of-These

Which hymn would you choose as a celebration of your life so far? Read (or sing) it. Use it as a prayer. Remember to listen to what God might be saying to you through it.
• Use this prayer of St Augustine to express your own relationship with God:

Late have I loved you, O beauty ever ancient, ever new. Late have I loved you and see, you were within and I outside, and outside I sought you. Misguided as I was I had only eyes for the appearance of beauty which you made. You were with me but I was not with you. Those things held me back from you, things whose only being was to be with you. You called; you cried; and you broke through my deafness. You flashed; you shone; and chased away my blindness. You became fragrant; I inhaled and sighed for you. I tasted and now hunger and thirst for you. You touched me and I burned for your embrace.

• Find a picture which you really like (not necessarily a religious one). Use it to listen and speak to God.

Jot down what happened in your journal or file.

Developing the conversation - guidelines

One of the questions often asked about all of this is "how do I know that what I am hearing or experiencing is really of God?" "How do I know I am not deluding myself?" Here are three guidelines we can use.

We can ask ourselves, is what I am thinking or experiencing in line with everything else I know about God and what the community of faith has said? So, to take an extreme example, if I think God is speaking to me asking me to steal from my employers so that I can give the money to charity I must ask myself is this in line with the tradition of the Church and is this in line with what I know about God. It is a classic "what would Jesus do" question.

Another guideline is that we can take advice from a trusted person. Sharing with another what is happening in our relationship with God can help us discern the truth. We have already seen that God often speaks to us through other people.

Thirdly we can ask whether what I am experiencing is producing a sense of rightness and peace in me or whether it is a sense of discomfort, leaving me ill at ease. St Ignatius of Loyola used an example to illustrate this. In those areas of my life where I am broadly following God's will, if my experience is calm and gentle, like water being soaked up by a sponge, it's a good sign that I can trust that it is truly God communicating with me. This can be true even when I'm being asked to do something quite difficult. However, if my experience is noisy and jarring, like water splashing on a stone, I might need to question more deeply whether this is, in fact, God leading me. Normally it's only when I'm going against what God wants of me that God's word will cut across and challenge me like this.

 ‹ Putting-It-All-Together Catholic spirituality says:

Our relationship with God is not one of equals. We are in dialogue with God, Father, Son and Spirit but at the same time our conversations are unique and intimate; conversations in which God calls us by name.

Conversing involves both listening and speaking. Both are essential in our prayer.

Our conversation with God brings us closer and helps us say "yes" to whatever is being asked of us. We may be faced with challenges to our way of life as a result of our prayer. We are called to action.

We can converse with the Lord anywhere, anytime.

We have resources through which the Lord speaks to us and through which we can respond. Among these, Scripture is a primary source but we also have a wealth of other treasures on which we can draw. These come from within our tradition and beyond.

We have some guidelines which we can employ to make sure we are not deluding ourselves.

◀ Pray-A-Psalm One of the greatest gifts the psalms offer to us is that they give us words to use when we are finding it difficult to express how we feel. Here are two psalms. The first is a wonderful psalm if all is going well for you. It is a prayer of thanksgiving the words of which we can use to speak to God of our gratitude. The second is part of psalm 88 which many people have found helpful when things are going or have gone wrong. It is a psalm of lament, the words of which we can use to speak to God of our pain and distress. Choose which one is right for you and pray it by reading it paragraph by paragraph leaving space in between each one and talking to God about what you have just read and what it means to you. If a section means little just wait a while and then move on.

A psalm of thanksgiving

O come let us sing to the Lord;
let us make a joyful noise to the rock of our salvation!
Let us come into his presence with thanksgiving;
let us make a joyful noise to him with songs of praise!

For the Lord is a great God, and a great king above all gods.
In his hands are the depths of the earth;
the heights of the mountains are his also.
The sea is his, for he made it, and the dry land,
which his hands have formed.

O come let us worship and bow down,
let us kneel before the Lord our maker.
For he is our God, and we are the people of his pasture,
the sheep of his hand.

(Psalm 95)

A psalm of lament

O Lord, God of my salvation, when at night,
I cry out in your presence, Let my prayer come before you;
incline your ear to my cry.
For my soul is full of troubles,
and my life draws near to Sheol.
I am counted among those who go down to the Pit;
I am like those who have no help,
like those forsaken among the dead,
like the slain that lie in the grave,
like those whom you remember no more,
for they are cut off from your hand...

My eye grows dim through sorrow.
Every day I call on you O Lord;
I spread out my hands to you.
Do you work wonders for the dead?
Do the shades rise up and praise you?
Is your steadfast love declared in the grave
or your faithfulness in Abaddon?
Are your wonders known in the darkness,
or your saving help in the land of forgetfulness?

But I, O Lord, cry out to you;
in the morning my prayer comes before you.
O Lord, why do you cast me off?
Why do you hide your face from me?
Wretched and close to death from my youth up
I suffer your terrors. I am desperate...

You have caused friend and neighbour to shun me;
my companions are in darkness.

◀ All-Together If you are using this book as part of a group here are some suggestions about how to share reflections on the contents of this chapter and what you might have discovered from it. Choose what suits your group.

- Share stories about how you converse with God.
- Can you think of other conversations Jesus had? Who were they with and what were they about?
- What did you make of the digging deeper section? Did anything strike you? Did anything confuse you? Talk it over in the group.
- Share what hymns and prayers are your own favourites and how they help you in your prayer.
- Ask one person to read slowly Isaiah 43:1-7. Ask a different group member to read it again. Have a short silence in which everyone chooses one word or phrase which has stood out for them. Each person shares their choice (just reading it out). When everyone has finished allow time for every one who wishes to share why they chose those words. This is a prayerful exercise so allow people to share without interruption.

Moving On

We have looked at different aspects of conversing with the Lord. We have also noted how that dialogue calls us to action; to share in the mission of Christ. Our spirituality turns us outwards as well as inwards and it is to that theme that we next turn.

5. Following

We looked in our last chapter at how we converse with the Lord. In this chapter we shall be looking at how important that conversation is in leading us to following the Lord as we live out our daily lives.

 ◄ Way-In These pictures show people pursuing different activities. They are typical of some of the things most of us do most days; working, shopping, leisure, looking after each other. Some of the activities we undertake each day because we have to, others we do for ourselves and some we do for the sake of other people; some are very active, others more passive, some we enjoy and others we loathe. Some are relatively straight-forward, others present us with real challenges. God's presence is there in all of them and we are called to respond.

But if in my life I fail completely to heed others, solely out of a desire to be "devout" and to perform my "religious duties" then my relationship with God will grow arid. It becomes merely "proper" but loveless.
Pope Benedict XVI

◄ Reflect-&-Jot Take time to think about your normal daily routine; the things you do. You might like to make a list or to draw a "map" of a typical day. What gives you energy and what saps it? Why? How do you normally respond to life's ups and downs. Make a note about this in your journal or file.

 ◂ Inside-The-Text We continue with our Gospel account of the conversation between Peter and Jesus. When we left it Jesus had asked Peter three questions and Peter had made his response. We continue now with a reminder of that last question.

Jesus said to him the third time, *"Simon, son of John, do you love me?"* Peter felt hurt because he said to him the third time *"Do you love me?"* He said to him *"Lord, you know everything; you know that I love you."* Jesus said to him, *"Feed my sheep. Very truly I tell you, when you were younger, you used to fasten your own belt and to go wherever you wished. But when you grow old, you will stretch out your hands, and someone else will fasten a belt around you and take you where you do not wish to go."* (He said this to indicate the kind of death by which he would glorify God.) After this he said to him, *"Follow me."* (*John* 21:17-19)

✎ ◀ Reflect-&-Jot Read the passage two or three times. In the two-way dialogue between Peter and Jesus, Peter professes his love for Jesus and is then challenged to follow him. As far as you can, try and put yourself in Peter's place. Note down what would be your reaction to what Jesus says to you.

◆ ◀ Digging-Deeper This conversation between Jesus and Simon Peter has come a long way from where it began.

> In the evening of life you will be examined in love.
> St John of the Cross, 1542-1591

Jesus has challenged Peter with the three questions. Twice he has asked if Peter really loved him. In Greek there are several words we translate in English with the one word, love, and the word used by Jesus in his first two questions is the strongest possible one (*agapan*). It was as if Jesus was asking, "Simon, do you really, really love me?" But Peter uses a different word for love in his reply (*philein*). His word does not have nearly such a strong force. It is as if Peter says, "Yes Lord, you know I really, really care deeply about you." Perhaps Peter is so acutely aware of how he has failed to really love in the past that he can't bring himself to give the assurances he fears he will never be able to keep.

> Jesus does not demand great actions from us but simply surrender and gratitude.
> St Thérèse of Lisieux, 1873-1897

This third question is different. This time Jesus switches from the "strong" word for love and uses the same "weaker" word Peter has used. It is almost as if he comes down to Peter's level and is saying, "I know your limitations. I'll meet you where you are." This is important for us because it says that, although we are called to give everything and to love to the uttermost, God knows perfectly well that our love is flawed and not as strong as it might be. Our spirituality is one which believes that however weak and full of holes our love may be it is enough for God to accept and use. It is to Peter, this person who denied his Lord and knows his own failings, that Jesus commands "Feed my sheep." God is not going to wait for him or us to reach a certain level of holiness before we're called to service. We cannot use our spiritual limitations as an excuse for not being ready to act.

Spirituality and Action

> To give our Lord perfect hospitality, Martha and Mary must combine.
> St Teresa of Avila, 1515-1582

The command to Peter to "Feed my sheep" is a particular and unique calling. He is to shepherd, tend and feed the flock that is the Church. But there is something else here that applies to every Christian. Peter is asked first to love the Lord and then feed the sheep. In the same way we are asked first to love and then to act. The love of God is the root of all the apostolic work that follows. It is at the basis of all our service. So we can say that our spirituality, our relationship with the Lord, fostered and fed by our listening and speaking to him, results in a life lived in both prayer and service for others. Our tradition points clearly to a belief that spirituality can never be totally inward looking. It can never be self-indulgent. Our inner life is always feeding and challenging the way we respond to the demands of life and the needs of others. And the need of the other is always being brought into our prayer. We are called to be both contemplative (looking at the Lord) and apostolic (serving the Lord). One demands the other. Without being fed by our inner life of prayer and time with the Lord, our service can become frazzled and a burden. We can get burnt out. Without service our prayer can become all about me; a self-seeking ego trip. This stress on the intimate connection between spirituality and service to the world is very strong in our tradition. It is at the root of our justice and peace work, our caring agencies and the work of many of our religious orders.

> Father, if someone comes to see me while I am at prayer, help me to see that, in leaving you to speak with this stranger, I am not leaving you at all.
> Walter Hilton, circa 1340-1396

Self giving love

As the passage unfolds Jesus has some strong words to say about the cost of this love. In effect Jesus says to Peter that, whereas previously he could make up his own mind about things and do what he wanted, in the future it will be very different. He will end up out of control of his own destiny and others will determine his fate. Humanly speaking it's a bleak prospect. We may well ask why anyone would want to put themselves in that position? It is one of the strange paradoxes of faith that it is when we are willing to give ourselves away that we truly find ourselves; that when we hand over our freedom to God we find we are most truly free. We sometimes discover this in little ways. For instance there is something quite joyful about discovering that my life is not just about me. I am somehow a much richer and fuller person when I give myself in service to others in some way or other. What lies at the heart of all this is self giving love. We are at a disadvantage here because our English word "love" has many meanings and connotations. We need to be clear that we are not talking about pleasant "lovely" feelings or even romantic love here. It is a loving *commitment* to

> Go forward in peace, for you have followed the good road. Go ahead without fear, for he who created you has made you holy, has always guided you, and loves you as a mother. Blessed be you, my God, for having created me.
> Clare of Assisi 1194-1253

his Lord that will be Peter's guiding force from now on, no matter where it leads him or whatever the cost. He knows he is loved steadfastly by his Lord and that mutual giving and receiving of love, shown in the back and forth conversation, is worth everything whatever the price may be. It is what our spirituality is all about, love of God and love of others.

The Paschal Mystery

We are not alone on this self giving path of committed love for the Lord which will lead us down paths both joyful and difficult. When we were baptised we became part of the body of Christ and we share in his life. He lives in us. This means that he acts in us and suffers in us and is alive in us. We call what Jesus did in his death and resurrection the paschal mystery. This we celebrate at every Mass and in union with him live out this mystery in our everyday lives. It is because Christ is alive in us, that we share in this mystery.

For Christians, salvation depends on a participation in the passion, death and resurrection of Christ, and on a direct personal relationship with God rather than on any technique.

Pontifical Council for Inter-religious Dialogue (Jesus the Bearer of the Water of Life, 4)

We often think of a mystery as a puzzle; something to be solved. The Christian understanding of mystery is different. It is an acknowledgement that, although something tremendous and beyond our complete understanding happens or is happening, we can glimpse and participate in that event. So, for instance, we know that when we are overcome with an experience that moves us to the very core, that experience is very real. Yet at the same time we can't quite explain it.

We can be taken out of ourselves by a spectacular view, or find the hair standing up on the back of our necks when we hear a particular piece of music but we cannot quite explain why. It is a mystery but most definitely real. The paschal mystery is similar to this. We can never fully understand the height and depth of the life-giving death and resurrection of Jesus yet we know it has changed everything for us. It lives deep in us and each time we find ourselves called to give ourselves unstintingly to others, or when we feel utterly defeated, or elated with joy, we share in that mystery because Christ lives and dies and is risen again in us. We are called to live out his self giving committed love in our own lives each and every day.

Adoration & Worship

We sometimes think of praise and adoration as merely telling God how wonderful he is. God is wonderful but adoring God is much more than telling him that. It is two things. It is an attitude of mind which acknowledges the supremacy of God. It locates God where God should be, at the root and summit of everything; at the centre of our lives. Secondly, our lives themselves give praise to God. When we live a life of self-giving love that itself is an act of adoration and worship. We see this in our Gospel passage. There we read that it is Peter's willingness to give his life for Jesus that glorifies God.

Fortunately most of us will not physically have to give up our lives for love of God, but we are all called to have this profligate self giving attitude. So each time we put our reputation on the line by standing up for an uncomfortable truth, or listen with attention to the same story we have heard someone tell us hundreds of times before; or day after day take on the burden of caring for the physical and emotional needs of an elderly relative, we are living out and incarnating the love of God which we ourselves know. We are sharing in the paschal mystery and glorifying God.

> He alone loves the Creator perfectly who manifests a pure love for his neighbour.
> St Bede the Venerable, 675-735

Follow me

This part of the narrative ends with the command of Christ, to "follow me." There is something very profound in the way this is recorded. Things happen in an ordered way. Jesus asks the big question first, do you love me? Next he commands Peter to *feed my sheep* then to *follow me*. This order is significant. Peter is called first to commit himself in love for his Lord. Out of this love he is to actively care for the flock. Finally he is reminded that he will only be able to care for the flock faithfully if he follows the way of Jesus. In other words it is only if he keeps his eyes on Jesus who is leading him that he can do what Jesus wants. If we are to follow the example of Peter it means that our spirituality is about keeping close to the Lord in order that we might hear what he wishes us to do. So the order is love the Lord first, hear the call to service and act on it and always keep following; listening and speaking to the one who loves us through thick and thin, whatever happens in our lives.

> If I have no contact whatsoever with God in my life, then I cannot see in the other anything more than the other, and I am incapable of seeing in him the image of God. But if in my life I fail completely to heed others, solely out of a desire to be devout and to perform my relgious duties, then my relationship with God will grow arid. It becomes merely proper, but loveless.
> Benedict XVI

So, spirituality is not about some esoteric religious practice, it is about loving, serving and following the Lord in our own unique circumstances. That means it is not about escaping from the world. Rather it is an exploration of what it means to love and be loved by God, and then to follow Christ with love in the world of today and in all the little things of life. We will look more at how we discern this path in our final chapter.

 ◀ Reflect-&-Jot Think for a while about your response to Jesus's question "Do you love me?"

- What word (or phrase) would you use in reply? Explore its various meanings in your journal.
- Recall and record a time when your faith cost you something. Why did you pay the price? If you cannot think of any such time don't feel guilty! Just as important is to think about what helps you remain faithful in the ups and downs of everyday.
- Gather together some photos or pictures or articles about people you think are serving Christ in different ways.
- What is most difficult for you about following Christ? You might find it helpful to do this by using just one word.

 ◀ Inside-Out

Intercessory Prayer

We have seen that prayer and service are both integral to what it means to follow Christ. Our spirituality also says that we serve one another by praying for each other and for the whole of God's world. We often call this intercessory prayer. We are quite right in asking God for what we and others need but it is helpful to remember a couple of things. When we pray in this way we do so understanding that God knows what is best for each one and that what we ask for may, or may not, be quite right. So, we pray for them knowing that God loves each person with a steadfast and intimate love and is never going to harm or do anything that is not for the best. Some people object that they have prayed for someone and God seemed to be deaf to their prayers. Sometimes it can seem that way but intercessory prayer is not about *us* telling God what we want but about holding the person or situation before God in trust and love.

Contemplative & Apostolic

This balance between the inner (what we might call "contemplative") and the outer ("apostolic"), aspects of our spirituality is not always easy to keep. Of course this balance may vary at different times in our lives depending on our circumstances. Nevertheless we should ask the question "is the balance right for me now?" We might find time for being with the Lord in order to hear how we are to follow him gets squeezed out of our busy schedules. We can always find something that, at the time, seems to be much more important to do. On the other hand it is also easy to say that we are not quite ready to "feed the sheep" and are ill-equipped, so we run into the escape route of "needing to be more spiritually ready". So how do we keep a balance? Here is one way using three criteria. We might think of it as having eyes looking in three directions at once.

Our eyes must, of course, be on God. Using the life and death and resurrection of Jesus is our "template". In our own situations to ask how he dealt with people, what he did and, above all the attitude he had towards them, can help us keep looking the right way. Taking time to reflect on his words and actions is a central part of our spirituality.

Our eyes must also be on the world in which we live and the circumstances in which we each live. We should expect (but we rarely do) to discover God there, inviting us to join in the task of building the Kingdom. That sounds very grand but, in reality, we help build the Kingdom every time love is exercised in however small a way. We do it when we care for someone; we do it when we affirm what is good and when we challenge what is wrong.

Our eyes also need to be on ourselves. That may sound wrong at first because we are aware that we should be looking away from ourselves to God. But asking God to help us see ourselves as we really are is helpful. Unless we are self-aware we may miss what God is saying to us and not hear the invitation he is issuing to us. So, in the context of being in the presence of God, we seek to open ourselves; to be more conscious of the call to love and the obstacles we sometimes put in the way that prevents us following and loving more deeply.

◀ Reflect-&-Jot Draw a circle like this in your journal or file

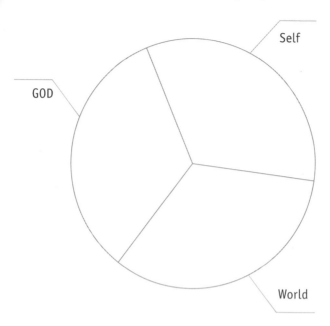

In each section jot down your responses to these three questions:

- What might I do to help me keep a closer eye on what I am being shown about God?
- What one thing might I do to help me see more clearly where God is active in the world in which I live?
- What one thing might I do to help me keep a closer eye on myself in relation to God?

Try-This

Think of someone you want to pray for. Sit with your hands resting gently, palms upwards, in your lap. Take a few minutes to remember that God is with you and present. Think about the person. Now, in the presence of God very slowly say their name. Give that person to God.

In our digging deeper section we said that our spirituality is about keeping close to the Lord in order that we might grow in love of him and hear what he wishes us to do. One way of doing this is through having some sort of review in the evening. It is a time when we can, in the presence of God, assess our loving and following at a deep level. This is sometimes called "The Review of the Day" or "The Examen".

This is not an examination in the sense of whether we pass a test or not, it is not even an examination of conscience. It is a way of looking closely at the day and to discern how we are doing and feeling. We are trying to hear what God is saying to us through our experiences and above all through what is going on deep within us. In this sense we are examining our motives and feelings; not the surface feelings but the movements and motives deep in our hearts. We need to be in touch at this level in order to sort out our reactions and not be blown about by them. Take your time over this.

- First of all spend a while just calming down and being still. Ask God to show you what has really been happening during the day.
- Slowly recall the day, allowing the moments which you enjoyed to emerge. Pause over these times and savour them. Ask God to show you what it was about these things that was enlivening. Then give thanks.
- Again, slowly recall the day, looking for those moments which were deadening, where you felt you were not at your best. What were the moods and feelings underlying these times. Ask God what is being revealed to you here. And then ask for forgiveness where you think you need it.
- Look forward. How do you feel as you face the next day? With apathy, fear, joy, distaste or excitement? Ask for God's help and entrust yourself and the future to God.

 ◄ Putting-It-All-Together Catholic spirituality says:

- A self giving committed love for God and for others is central to our lives.
- Christ lives in us and so we live out the life, death and resurrection, the paschal mystery, in our own lives.
- God is at work, loving us in the deep inner core of each of us so that our love for him and others can grow.
- Our inner life, hidden with Christ, and the outer manifestation of that relationship are two sides of one coin; they are inseperable.
- Our spirituality is both contemplative and apostolic, we are called to keep looking at the Lord and at the needs of others.
- Working for a better world, building the Kingdom and caring for others, is a non-negotiable element of our spirituality.
- Praying for others is part of our service to them.
- God does not wait for us to reach a certain level of holiness before calling us to act.

◀ Pray-A-Psalm This psalm expresses several things. It is a thanksgiving for God's ever-present love and a prayer that we may stay close to God in good times and bad. Read it prayerfully and see what aspect of the psalm means most to you. Make it your own prayer by using your own words to express to God what it says to you.

Incline your ear O Lord, and answer me,
for I am poor and needy.
Preserve my life, for I am devoted to you;
save your servant who trusts in you.
You are my God.
Teach me your way O Lord, that I may walk in your truth
give me an undivided heart to revere your name.
I give thanks to you O Lord my God
with my whole heart, and I will glorify your name for ever.
For great is your steadfast love towards me;
you have delivered my soul from the depths of Sheol.
O God the insolent rise up against me;
a band of ruffians seeks my life,
and they do not set you before them.
But you O Lord, are a merciful God
and gracious, slow to anger
and abounding in steadfast love and faithfulness.
Turn to me and be gracious to me;
give your strength to your servant;
save the child of your serving maid.
Show me a sign of your favour,
so that those who hate me may see it
and be put to shame, because you,
Lord, have helped me and comforted me.

(Psalm 86:1-2, 11-17)

◀ All-Together If you are using this book as part of a group here are some
suggestions about what you might do when you come together.

- Share what you have gained from working through this chapter. Has anything surprised or disturbed you?
- Think of people you know, or know of, who are shining examples of the paschal mystery being lived out. Share what it is about them that strikes you.
- Make a group list of all the ways your members try to serve others. Where does your life of prayer fit in to your life of service?
- If you don't already have one, start an intercession book in the parish in which people can write requests for prayer (or have an intercession board).
- When Jesus says "Follow me" what does that mean to you?
- Ask someone to read 1 Corinthians 13 (Paul's well known hymn to love) slowly and carefully. In the light of what this passage says about love, what does it mean to hear Jesus say "Do you love me"? Share your responses.

Moving On

We have seen how our spirituality is about following Christ in our love of God and service of others. Keeping the conversation going and staying close helps us choose the unique path God wishes us to follow. How spirituality helps us discern that path and shape our lives through the choices we make will be the theme of our next chapter.

5. Choosing

Introduction

Following the Lord and keeping close to him in love was the theme of our last chapter. Anyone who takes following Christ seriously soon discovers that there are choices to be made; choices about how we are to grow in our relationship with God and choices about how God calls us to follow each and every day. Our spirituality helps us discern how to make those choices wisely.

> United with Jesus and with the power of his Holy Spirit, we can surrender our will to him and decide to choose what the Son has always chosen; to do what is pleasing to the Father.
>
> *Catechism of the Catholic Church*, 2825

 ◀ Way-In Here are some pictures which show people making a choice.

Notice some of these show "big" choices and some appear to be less so. We make choices each day, some are relatively minor (what to wear, what to have for a meal this evening etc). Some choices can radically effect our way of life. For instance deciding about how to react to someone who has hurt us deeply, should we hold a grudge and ignore them or to try and re-engage with them? Still other choices are life changing such as which career to choose, whether or not to get married and to whom, whether to give up the house and move into sheltered accommodation. Sometimes we get the choices right, sometimes we don't.

 ◀ Reflect-&-Jot Take time to think about some of the choices you have made in your own life. You might like to make a list of the big ones. Some you may wish to rejoice over in which case take a moment to thank God. Perhaps you regret some of them. If you do, resist the temptation to pass harsh judgement on yourself. Just quietly offer them to God. Record your conversation with the Lord in some way.

◀ Inside-The-Text Here is the final part of our chapter from St John's Gospel. Peter has been told by Jesus that he is to feed the sheep and to follow him. Here is what happens next.

Peter turned round and saw the disciple whom Jesus loved following them; he was the one who had reclined next to Jesus at the supper and had said, *"Lord, who is it that is going to betray you?"* When Peter saw him he said to Jesus, *"Lord, what about him?"* Jesus said to him, *"If it is my will that he remain until I come, what is that to you? Follow me!"*
(John 21:20-22)

So far the conversation between Peter and Jesus has been the intimate dialogue between the two of them. Now a third person, the one we call the beloved disciple, is indirectly involved. The conversation continues but that close back and forth dialogue seems to have taken a different turn. Peter has other concerns.

◀ Reflect-&-Jot Read the Gospel passage again. Jot down what you make of it.

◀ Digging-Deeper

Turning away and turning back

Lord God, in your mercy do not look on what I am now, nor on what I have been, but on what I desire to be.
The Cloud of Unknowing, late fourteenth century

The first thing we can note occurs in the first two words, "Peter turned". He turns round and sees someone other than Jesus. In so doing he knows Jesus is still there and the conversation is still going on but his attention shifts somewhere else and, as a result, he takes his eyes off the Lord. Just when he should be thinking about what it will mean to follow his Lord in the future he is asking a question about the future of someone else! Of course, we may be doing Peter a disservice and his question about the future of the other disciple may be one of genuine concern, but nevertheless keeping the focus on Christ is the principle foundation of our spirituality. In him we see what the love of God for us is like and we are called to focus on him alone and not spend our energies trying to second-guess what God is up to. Most of us find that quite difficult to do. It is a spirituality which requires an attitude of trustful surrender. Something we will look at a little later.

Prayer is not asking. Prayer is putting oneself in the hands of God…and listening to his voice in the depths of our hearts.
Blessed Mother Teresa, 1910-1997

Peter has seen this disciple "whom Jesus loved". He is important here because he is what we are called to be. He is often referred to as "the beloved disciple" and tradition associates him with John. He occurs in the Gospel as the one who is always close to Jesus. At the Last Supper it is he who is next to Jesus and he is the only one of the male disciples who stands at the foot of the cross when all others have fled. This disciple stands for every Christian. We are all called to be the beloved disciple, invited to recline next to Jesus and later to stand at the foot of the cross. Our spirituality is aimed at helping us do just that.

Being and remaining with Christ through all our ups and owns is one of the most difficult things we try to do but it is t the centre of our spirituality. We know that being close to od is exactly what we deeply long for yet we can sometimes eel that we are utterly unable to be there. We believe we are ot worthy or that we are not capable of it. We get distracted r we don't seem to be getting anywhere so we think we've ailed or we give up altogether believing it is just too hard. Ve want so much to get closer to God but we find ourselves opelessly inadequate. The problem here is that we are doing he equivalent of what Peter did, we are *looking in the wrong direction*. We are looking at something (probably ourselves) ather than at the Lord who never gives up on us. When we ealise this we also recognise that we have a choice. We can urn back and start again or we can give up in despair. There s a technical word for this turning back to God. We call it conversion. To be converted literally means to "turn around"; o face God once more. It is not something we do just once but something we are called to do over and over again. So, even if ve turn away it is always possible to turn back. Perhaps that is vhat happened to Peter. We don't know but the strong words of Jesus saying, in effect, "it's nothing to do with you what I plan for this disciple, you are to follow me" brings forth no response from Peter. He is silent. It is almost as if these words from Jesus bring him up short.

Discerning the will of God

The future for this beloved disciple does seem to worry Peter. Perhaps it is a normal human reaction to want to know or to worry about someone else's fate, especially as Peter has just heard about his own. But Jesus turns the attention away from this and back to the task in hand. He talks about his will. ("If it is my will that he remain until I come what is that to you. Follow me.") Peter is to concentrate on following God's will in his own life, not on that of another. One of the most important elements of spirituality is how it enables us to discern what God's will is for ourselves. But what do we mean by God's will? We sometimes think of this in a rather fatalistic way - what will be, will be. It might be more helpful to look at God's will as something much more active. "To will" is a verb, it's a "doing" word. So God's will is God's action, God's work. What God does (wills) for us is to shape us into people

Christ's call to conversion continues to resound in the lives of Christians… St Peter's conversion after he had denied his master three times bears witness to this.
Catechism of the Catholic Church, 1428

And when we have fallen, through frailty or blindness, then our courteous Lord touches us, stirs and calls us. And then he wills that we should see our wretchedness and humbly acknowledge it. But it is not his will that we should stay like this, nor does he will that we should busy ourselves too much with self-accusation, nor is it his will that we should despise ourselves. But he wills that we should quickly turn to him.
Julian of Norwich, b. 1342

When thoughts of this or that come I turn and say: "Only what you will my God."
Blessed Mary MacKillop,
1842-1909

We are at Jesus's disposal. If he wants you to be sick in bed, if he wants you to proclaim his work in the street, if he wants you to clean the toilets all day, that's all right. Everything is alright. We must say "I belong to you. You can do whatever you like." This is our strength and this is the joy of the Lord.
Blessed Mother Teresa, 1910-1997

Lord, who made me and all my limbs, give me grace to serve you with all my limbs employed in your service, constantly bending as you direct me, constantly ready to move or rest at your command.
Richard Rolle, 1290-1349

who are fully alive. We need to discern how God is going about that activity in us so that we can co-operate with that will. In order to do this we have to make choices. We are not automatons, God wants us to choose but our choices are to be made in the context of what it means to follow Christ who came to give us life in all its fullness. (*John* 10:10) Making choices that are in accordance with what God wants for us is very much part of spirituality. In classical terms we call this discerning God's will for our lives. Discerning is not something we do only at those times when we are faced with the big choices in life. It is also about discerning how we are to live in the here and now each and every day.

We do not know how Peter reacts when Jesus, yet again, commands him to concentrate his attention on the task of following. The choice for him, and for us, is between following Christ and following something or someone else. We live in a society where choice is everywhere and we are very fortunate to be in such a situation. Making wise choices can be extremely difficult with such a bewildering array of options on offer. It is even harder because our society tends to say one choice is as valid as another. So how can our spirituality help us make the sort of choices which are in line with the work of God and bring us more and more into that fullness of life we are offered? Before we look at that let's reflect on what has been said so far.

◀ Reflect-&-Jot Think about a time when you have turned away from God and then turned back. What difference has that experience made to you since?

If you are a visual sort of person choose a colour which expresses turning away and one which expresses turning back.

Find some photographs or write a paragraph or two which express where and when you have discovered God at work in your life (God's will for you) in the past.

 ◀ Inside-Out

Turning around

We have already discovered that our spiritual journey is not undertaken on our own. As we develop in our relationship with God and other people, one of the ways we can discern if we have made a less than wise choice is to share it with a trusted person. God can and does use other people to help us see things more clearly. If we do discern that need to turn around, one of the treasures the Church offers to us is the opportunity to acknowledge our wrong choices. The Sacrament of Reconciliation is really a sacrament which celebrates our conversion, our turning around. As such it not only assures us of God's forgiveness it marks a new beginning in our discipleship. Over the centuries faithful members of the Church have grappled with how to discern God's will in their lives so there is a collective wisdom on which we can draw.

On the next page are some ways we may find helpful. They are not in any particular order except the first really does come first! You may like to make a copy of them and keep them somewhere (perhaps in your journal) so that you can look at them when necessary. Each one has a handy question at the end which it may be helpful to ask when faced with a choice.

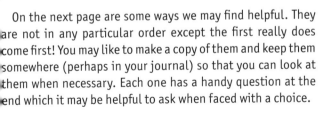

Making good choices

- **Keep it simple.** At the root of our spirituality we try to keep before us the desire to live a life in the footsteps of Christ and that lies at the heart of all our choices. So we can ask ourselves *"If I choose this path will it lead me closer to Christ or not?"*

- **Look at the choices others have made.** We can consider what choices people in the past have made, especially if they have been in a similar situation to our own. Sometimes we will find the experience of such people recorded in the pages of our Scriptures and sometimes in the lives of the saints. So we can ask ourselves *"What light does their experience shed on my own? Do they offer me clues about what direction to take or what option to choose?"*

- **Choices are made within a context not in the abstract.** Usually there are many different factors which come into play. Collect all the necessary information and take a hard headed look at concrete demands of the present situation. So we can ask ourselves *"What are the demands of the current situation, the people and the context I am in?"*

- **We can think about the effects on those around us.** We have to take into account our responsibilities and commitments to others. They have to be part of the reckoning too. God wants us to use our common sense as well as our faith. So we can ask ourselves, *"How will the choice affect those around me?"* What are the pros and cons of the choice before us?

- **We can look at what is going on within ourselves.** Listening to our own inner voice is important. Perhaps we feel unease about what might be the outcome of a possible course of action. If so, the task then is to see if that discomfort is coming because we are being challenged to change or because we think the change would lead us down the wrong road and away from the path of following Christ. So we can ask ourselves *"Will this choice free me in my inner self or enslave me?"*

- **We need to recognise our blind spots.** We can all make mistakes so we do well to look at our previous experience. We all carry baggage from the past and sometimes experience shows us what is or what isn't the right path to choose. So we can ask, *"What are my strengths and what are my weaknesses?"*

- **Share with a trusted person.** This enables us to test out our thoughts and responses. So we can ask *"Who might I talk to about the choices I make?"*

- **Imagine.** What advice would you give to someone else who was in the same position as you?

Checking it out

How will we know when we have made a choice in line with the will of God? We can say that there are some things that stand out as the characteristics of good choices. We shall know we have probably made a right choice if these criteria are evident:

• Good choices never isolate us from other people.

• Good choices lead to human flourishing.

• Good choices are about generosity of spirit.

• Good choices give us a sense of "rightness".

• Good choices help us to see things in a new and life giving way.

• Good choices help us deal with our inner demons.

• Good choices help us live in a more integrated way.

Of course we can never be one hundred percent sure when we make a decision that, in the end, it will turn out as we thought. Even if, with hindsight, we can see that the choice was not right, if we made it in good faith we should not blame ourselves. God will still be working in us. Like Peter we can humbly acknowledge what has happened to us and move on.

Surrender to God

In order to make choices this way we need to be open and to have an attitude of trust that God will show us the way. One of the constant refrains in our spiritual tradition is that of surrender to God. Surrender in this context is not about being a doormat or giving up the struggle. It is about being really open-hearted in the presence of God and pondering things with no concern except whether it is what God wants. Whatever God wants is going to be life giving in some way.

Few souls understand what God would accomplish in them if they were to abandon themselves unreservedly to him and if they were to allow his grace to mould them accordingly.
St Ignatius of Loyola, 1491-1556

The Spirit's Presence

Every time we begin to pray to Jesus it is the Holy Spirit who draws us on the way of prayer…that is why the Church invites us to call on the Holy Spirit every day, especially at the beginning and end of every important action.

Catechism of the Catholic Church, 2670

Most of us struggle to be that open in our prayer but there is no cause for despair here because we are not even asked to attempt this surrender to God relying on our own strength. We cannot possibly hope to achieve this openness with God through our own efforts alone. St Paul reminds us of this when he talks about how the Spirit is with us in our prayer. "The spirit too comes to help us in our weakness. For when we cannot choose words in order to pray properly, the Spirit himself, expresses our plea in a way that could never be put into words, and God who knows everything in our hearts, knows perfectly well what he means, and that the pleas of the saints, expressed by the Spirit are according to the mind of God." (*Romans* 8:26-27).

So the Spirit is within us, praying in us and helping us through what we call the Spirit's gifts - gifts of wisdom, understanding, counsel and fortitude; knowledge, piety and fear of the Lord. If, in the power of the Spirit, we can surrender to God no matter how fitfully and poorly, our choices will in fact be being made from that deep core in us which is where God is at work. That such choices have been soundly made is likely to be confirmed by what are called 'fruits of the Spirit' - charity and joy, peace and patience, kindness and generosity, gentleness and faithfulness.

Try-This

- Take time to settle down. Ask the Spirit to be with you as you pray.
- Consider quietly the word "follow". Think about it and think round it. Try and see it from every angle. Take your time.
- Now leave the word in your mind but try to open your heart to God. Don't try to say anything. Every time you find yourself distracted just repeat the word "follow" a few times. Stay with the process as long as seems right.
- Thank God for the time and commit yourself to following the Lord in whatever way you choose.
- If you found this a helpful process remember you can use whatever word you wish as the focus for your time with the Lord.

 ◀ Reflect-&-Jot Think of a choice you made recently. It doesn't have to be a very "big" choice but something of importance to you. Using the criteria above note down how you now feel about the choice you made?

◄ Putting-It-All-Together Catholic spirituality says:

Turning away is possible but so is turning back. We are called to conversion over and over again.

Making choices is part of our spiritual life because the choices we make help us conform (or not conform) to the fullness of life God wants for us and others. This is God's will for us.

We have a rich treasury to draw on to help us hear how God is calling us to discern the right path.

Discerning God's will requires an attitude of surrender to the God who always wills our good.

The Holy Spirit is within us and prays within us especially when we don't know how to express in words what is deep within us.

◄ Pray-A-Psalm Psalm 23 (The Lord is my Shepherd) is such a familiar psalm to many of us that we can easily gloss over it. It is used so often at weddings and funerals that our ears can become dulled to the message of openness which it conveys. It eloquently shows the psalmist's relationship with the Lord to be one of intimate surrender to, and trust in, the God of Israel. We can make that prayer our own. Spend some time getting settled and ready. Read the psalm right through slowly. Then read each section stopping after each one to reflect on what the words mean in your relationship with God.

The Lord is my shepherd I shall not want.
He makes me to lie down in green pastures;
he leads me beside still waters; he restores my soul.
He leads me in the right paths for his name's sake.

Even though I walk through the darkest valley,
I fear no evil; for you are with me;
your rod and your staff, they comfort me.

You prepare a table before me in the presence of my
enemies; you anoint my head with oil, my cup overflows.

Surely goodness and mercy shall follow me all the days
of my life, and I shall dwell in the house of the Lord
my whole life-long.

◀ All-Together If you are using this book as part of a group here are some suggestions about how to share reflections on the contents of this chapter and what you might have discovered from it. Choose what suits your group.

- Share together anything from this chapter which has struck you.
- Share some stories about the choices you have had to make in your life. How did you go about making them and how did your prayer help you in making your decision?
- Imagine you have to evacuate your home in five minutes time and you can only take three things in a small bag with you. What would you choose and why? What criteria will you use to make your decision?
- Use the psalm and let each group member share what each of the sections means in their relationship with God. Listen prayerfully to each person's contribution without interruption.

Moving On

Our pondering of the passage in John's Gospel has almost come to an end. There is one final verse that concludes both the chapter and the whole Gospel.

But there are many other things that Jesus did; if every one of them were written down, I suppose that the world itself could not contain the books that would be written. (*John* 21:25)

They are fitting words with which to conclude our exploration of Catholic spirituality. There are many other things that could be said about all that Jesus does in our lives that are not in this book. It was never the intention of this publication to cover everything, but we hope both the guidelines provided here and the suggestions for different ways to deepen the relationship with God, will be something you can take into the future. From that base other aspects of the Christian faith and life not covered here can be considered.

As the Gospel ends, Peter is only just starting the next stage of his life. The question of Jesus to Peter "Do you love me?" is made repeatedly to each of us throughout our lives. We hope this book has helped you in your own relationship with the Lord and in your own response to that question.

Inside images:

12 Standing on a rock by the sea © Przemyslaw Szablowski.

14 Fishing nets © Holbox.

21 Meadow in Kananaskis Country in Alberta, Canada © BGSmith. Diverse family © Tracy Whiteside. Hot air balloon © topseller.

22 Fisherman scoops fish © withGod.

26 Hostiam Sanctam, Feast of Corpus Christi © Lawrence Lew,OP. Theatrical representation of Passion and death of Jesus Christ in the village of Alcorisa © Bykofoto/Shutterstock.com.

27 From the film The Passion of the Christ, Jim Caviezel © picture-alliance/KPA Honorar & Belege. Jesus praying and talking, Passion of Jesus in Trafalgar Square © Mazur/catholicchurch.org.uk. The Last Supper World Youth Day 2008 © Mazur/catholicchurch.org.uk.

28 The Annunciation, Peter Paul Rubens, St John's Church or Janskerk © Renata Sedmakova/Shutterstock.com

29 St Gianna Beretta Molla, Vatican City State by Vincenzo Pinto/Getty Images. St Anthony of Padua with child Jesus © Zvonimir Atletic/Shutterstock.com.

33 Two bored businessmen © PathDoc/Shutterstock.com. Meeting in coffee shop © Monkey Business Images Shutterstock.com. Olympic Mass in Westminster Cathedral © Mazur/catholicnews.org.uk.

34 Fish on a wooden skewer © Alexander Tihonov.

41 Holy Communion , World Youth Day 2011 © Mazur/catholicchurch.org.uk.

44 Diner party outdoors © bikeriderlondon.

45 Older person chatting © Shutterstock.com. Architects Meeting © Monkey Business Images.

46 Feeding a lamb © daseaford.

48 Clifton Pilgrimage To The Holy Land © Mazur/catholicchurch.org.uk.

59 Athlete running © lzf. Business meeting © wavebreakmedia. Shopping cart at supermarket © Blend Images

60 Crucifixion of Jesus Christ detail © Photosebia.

64 Eucharistia © Lawrence Lew OP.

67 Olympic Mass in Westminster Cathedral © Mazur/catholicnews.org.uk.

72 Prayer vigil honouring Pope John Paul II © Mazur/catholicchurch.org.uk. Girl cooking © Shutterstock.com Choosing a shirt © Nejron Photo. Bride and groom © Halfpoint.

74 The Last Supper © Antonio Gravante.

78 Passion of Jesus in Trafalgar Square © Mazur/catholicchurch.org.uk.

79 Spirit in the City confession in Leicester Square © Mazur/catholicnews.org.uk.